Book Cover Painting— *"Happiness"*—Emanuel Nkuranga

Emanuel is part of an upcoming promising generation of contemporary Rwandan artists and did not hesitate to lend his art to this project.

Emanuel's work can be seen at http://www.devearts.com/emmanuel-nkuranga.html or he can be contacted at emmamain23@gmail.com.

WHAT PEOPLE ARE SAYING ABOUT "MOMENTS"

"I once read that the universe is made of stories, not atoms. We are therefore all connected by the stories we tell. In **"Moments: A Poetic Heart Journey"** Dawn tells her story of her quest for God, and in a very real sense, God's quest for her.

The poetry I love most makes me feel the condition of another, and these poems make you sit forward with a chill creeping up your spine, and images visualizing in your mind. Her poems, her story, carry us to the extremes of sorrow and unexpected joy, even as we search for meaning in this world under sin's curse.

Dawn has been a member of my church for almost four years, and has made an indelible impression on our church family and me in a number of significant ways. She is a deeply spiritual woman with a compelling story of God's unconditional love being the reason for her amazing life. Her insightful contributions even in casual conversations have delighted me over the years.

I think the author can be confident there will be many grateful readers, who will have gained a broader perspective on how God sometimes works in circuitous ways, to bring about an abiding trust in his eternal providences in our lives.

I am therefore confident that this timeless literary work will have a lasting, redemptive impact on generations to come."

-- Abraham Julius Jules, D.Min, Pastor
Mt. Vernon SDA Church, Mt. Vernon, NY, USA
Co-Author, *"A Guide to Effective Pastoral Ministry"*

"This book is as much intriguing as it is inspiring. Dawn bravely, yet tenderly, grapples with some of the greatest challenges of our time such as love, discipline, brokenness, restoration and social responsibility.

These poems will bring tears to yours eyes; but, they will also flood you with peace, joy and hope as you see the unconditional love of God who alone restores and gives new beginnings to all who have experienced brokenness, rejection, abuse, self-doubt and feel like they can never love again. You will find the interactive style of this book to be quite engaging and life transforming.

"Moments" *flows from a heart laid bare by God's unconditional love and a life full of joy unspeakable. That is who I have known Dawn to be as my wife and I interacted with her and other Christian young people in Johannesburg. I have learnt that one is not free until one starts living and loving without masking. Dawn is a heart unmasked by love—God's love.*

I strongly recommend this life-changing work to all who seek to know how to rise above their life situations and find a complete new life through a relationship with Christ that is fulfilling, exciting and transforming; to all who desire to know their true identity and destiny; and, to all who love everything beautiful and with happy endings."

-- Samuel Misiani, Pastor

Amazing Grace SDA Church, Johannesburg, South Africa

Author, *"Sweeter Than Honey: The Awesome Favour of God!"*

"This work of creative excellence has truly captivated my own heart—emotions and all!

It is reflective of the person I met many years ago in Barbados; an extraordinarily talented, gifted and creative woman. I am thrilled to see how Dawn has honed her skills to produce a work of art which is reflective of her authenticity and passion as a God-seeker. Her versatility and intellectual acumen in juxtaposing the genres of poetry and prose to challenge us to take a personal journey, where we line up our heart with God's heart, is indeed awesome.

Dawn's ability to share deep theological messages, packaged as they have been, attests to her God-given creative genius. She is indeed God's poet.

I am delighted, beyond measure, to endorse this outstanding literary work, which I am sure, will give birth to more children of God.

I am particularly pleased with the work form the point of view of being a teacher of literature and language for almost 35 years. This is great stuff!"

-- Nola Estwick, BA, Senior Teacher
Christ Church Foundation School, Barbados

"The huge smile on her face reflects the season in her life. She has found her place in the heart of God. Dawn lives, laughs and loves freely because of her confident relationship with her Father, God.

Having been her personal pastor, shepherd and spiritual counselor for more than two decades, I have observed her transition from religiosity to spirituality; from trying to be successful to endeavoring to be faithful. Dawn's faithfulness has granted her a place in God's heart.

This book is engaging and well-written. And, you will be drawn closer to Christ and to experience the heart of God as a result of reading it."

-- Steve D. Cassimy, D.Min
Ministerial Secretary & Family Ministries Director
Greater New York Conference of SDAs, USA
Co-Author, *"A Guide to Effective Pastoral Ministry"*

"It has been a joyful pleasure to read this fascinating and thought-provoking book.

Dawn, with ease, took me on an exciting journey as she chronicled some of her experiences and encounters of life. She passionately shared from her heart. The book challenges us to learn to pay attention to the moments of life rather than contemplating life in its entirety.

Through a highly engaging writing style, Dawn provides an incisive analysis of the concept of "moments". Her moments taught her to be Christ-like, to have a better understanding of God, and see Him do miracles in her life.

It is evident that a knowledge of God at an early age implanted long-lasting roots which enabled her to have stayed her journey with God.

The book provides a practical, reasonable and justifiable rationale for a relationship with one's fellowmen and with God."

-- Daviceto A. C. Swaby, D.Min, Pastor
Kingston SDA Church, Ontario, Canada

MOMENTS

MOMENTS
A Poetic Heart Journey

Dawn A. Minott, MA

Edited by Dr. Ahmed N. Reid, PhD

Order this book online at www.trafford.com
or email orders@trafford.com

Most Trafford titles are also available at major online book retailers.

Printed in the United States of America.

ISBN: 978-1-4669-7772-3 (sc)
ISBN: 978-1-4669-7773-0 (hc)
ISBN: 978-1-4669-7774-7 (e)

Library of Congress Control Number: 2013902092

Trafford rev. 02/13/2013

www.trafford.com

North America & international
toll-free: 1 888 232 4444 (USA & Canada)

phone: 250 383 6864 ♦ fax: 812 355 4082

To my Mother
Agnes Elizabeth Burke

*For letting me go so I could test
the wings you gave me.*

"When death finds you,
hope that it finds you alive".
(Japanese proverb)

FOREWORD

"*On* an age and time where poetry and prose of the heart are slowly being replaced with musical thumps wrapped in loud beats which demand our undivided attention; in this maze of 'hurried busyness', it's sometimes hard to pay close attention to 'words' which invite us to pause and reflect.

These special gifts are given to each of us to use wisely as tools which comfort, correct, convict, command, commend while soothing the soul.

Such are the word-gifts presented here from the very special and pure heart space of Dawn Minott.

In this special collection of prose, poems and prayers wrapped in carefully selected words, Dawn Minott invites us, the readers, to take a moment and drink from her pool of life experiences. Her words here challenge each of us as the reader to dig deeper while looking a bit more honestly at the life we've been given to experience right here, right now.

Through Dawn's work we are invited to get on the road that leads to our very own custom, tailor-made journey designed by the God of Abraham, Isaac and Jacob and the One who is desirous of being your God too."

—Gail Masondo, Author, *"Now This Feels Like Home"*

PREFACE

As you will readily see, I've used prose, poetry and prayer to communicate the message of *"Moments: A Poetic Heart Journey"*. My purpose for writing this book, however, goes beyond composing a literary work focused on exaggerated piety or religious zeal; and, is more than an imaginative awareness of experiences expressed through rhythmic language choices to evoke an emotional response. Rather, this book is a candid exposé of lessons being learnt on my journey to knowing the heart of God. Lessons predicated on debunking the widely-held misconception that we only live once to heralding the actuality that we, in fact, die at least once but we live every day.

You will also notice that I've used a very personal and engaging style in communicating and inviting you to share your own heart-journey. However, this is not a "self-help" book because the fundamental purpose of this book is to invite you to not only live life; but, to HAVE abundant life and attaining that is more than you are capable of helping yourself to do.

If you are familiar with the maxims of Jesus Christ (Saint John 10:10), you may have quickly realized that what has inspired the purpose for writing this book is aligned to the ultimate motive of Christ's mission—to move humanity from the life that we can live to the life we can HAVE. My intent is to arouse in each reader a desire to conceptualize their best-lived life and to live that life each day as if the next will not come. But, more significantly, to move a step further and visualize the benefits and joys of their best-lived life compounded exponentially and to know with full assurance that that abundant-life envisioned can be their reality.

Each life-journey will end, but one that is lived with the intent of knowing the heart of God is one that will be abundantly lived. If this book evokes a desire in you to HAVE life—to possess, enjoy, exhibit life abundantly—and not just to merely live, breathe, exist or survive, then I would have achieved the primary purpose for sharing heart-moment extracts from my interminable heart-journey to know the heart of God.

ACKNOWLEDGEMENTS

*F*irst and above all, I thank God for His blessings and partnership for this was a **God & Dawn Incorporated** project.

I also take this opportunity to express my profound gratitude and heartfelt regards to those without whom this project would not have been realized.

My Family: mom, Agnes; father, Lloyd; aunty Cherry; uncle Kenneth; my siblings Nerissa, Stephen, Patrick, Lisa, Tanya, Bruce and their spouses; and my nieces and nephews for being my anchor. No matter where I roam you all will always be my "home".

My Motivators: Terrence Harrison, Mark Hutchinson, Alton Grizzle, Anthony Fagan, Veronica Mahiga, Georgette Henry-Whyte for unending encouragement, constant prayers, and ceaseless affirmation.

My Spiritual Mentors & Shepherds: Nola Estwick, Gail Masondo, Andrew Adar; Pastors Cassimy, Jules, Misiani and Swaby for keeping me grounded in my faith and in the word of God.

My Sister-/Aunty-Friends: Marvette Facey, Donna Singh, Amanda Khoza, Harriet Yearwood, Estee Barends, Sandra Abrahams, Nichole Bernard; and my Daddy's-girl sister in ministry, Ayanda Mnkeni, for being my global support system.

Dr. Ahmed N. Reid: for your guidance, support and the generous gift of time in proof-reading and editing.

Emanuel Nkuranga: for the complimentary use of your art work, *"Happiness"*.

CONTENTS

*W*elcome! I am very pleased you chose to embark on this journey with me.

It is a very personal journey; a journey of self-discovery. A journey in which you will vicariously travel through prose, poetry and prayer to experience how God pursued me and won my heart with His patient-undying-don't-want-anything-in-return love. It is a life-journey—a poetic-autobiography.

It is an imaginative journey wherein you will experience moments when the Divine Poet partnered with me to inspire a thought, germinate it in my mind and birthed it into creative expressions. Expressions captured in words, rhythm and rhyme and expressed as epic, lyric, narrative, ode and ballads.

It is a commemorative journey. Each poem memorializes the moments when the Almighty God contained the enormity of His "Godness" to make possible this divine-human artistic partnership that resulted in the creation of poetic expressions, dated for posterity and categorized as *Familial Moments, Moments of Self-Discovery, Moments of Encouragement, God Moments* and *Miraculous Moments.*

It is a guided journey. Each poem is prefaced with "Before Word"—a prosaic elucidation revealing its dawning; and punctuated with "Nevertheless Afterward . . ."—a pause at poignant moments in acknowledgment that *"no chastening for the present seems to be joyous, NEVERTHELESS, AFTERWARD it yields the peaceable fruit of righteousness unto them which are exercised thereby".* (Hebrews 12:11, King James Version)

It is a contemplative journey. You are invited to a space of personal reflection through "Heart-Poem" which is first a conversation from my heart to God's then from your heart to His. The journey is concluded with the "Heart-to-Heart".

I invite you to make this your journey to the heart of God as well. And, at the end of your sojourn, it is my desire that you will be blessed exceedingly-abundantly-above all that you expected.

Welcome to *"Moments: A Poetic Heart Journey"*

INTRODUCTION

Before Word—Part I

Why Prose, Poetry & Prayer?

I have always been a lover of words and in artistically arranging them in simple and conversational forms to make declarations. However, what I could not voice aloud I wrote. I used varying tones and pace in structuring words to communicate the experiences of life—its ups and downs, its joys and challenges, its victories and defeats, its successes and failures.

On this journey to the heart of God, prayer has become my mainstay. I've learned to pray about everything, from the minutest to the most grandiose of issues like: *"Dear God, please help me find the keys"* to *"Dear God, the doctor thinks it's cancerous, please let this biopsy be benign"*. I've prayed through my doubts, strengthening myself in the Lord. I've prayed through my tears, encouraging myself in the Lord. I've prayed through my weakest moments, emboldening myself in the Lord. In time, I found people made more and more requests of me to pray so I've stood in the gap on their behalf. I've offered prayer like a gift—sometimes I prayed with people in the moment that the request was made, other times I interceded privately on their behalf and I've even sent prayers via the Internet.

I love to pray and I love to write. However, I don't just love to write, I love to write poems.

My appreciation for the poetic art form stems from the creative license it affords me to not only manipulate words, but to also express these words through recital and declaration. This love was made even stronger when I pondered God's use of words in the creative process. In essence, God spoke—He made declarations—and the universe and all it contains appeared. I can't resist but to exercise creative license and dramatize this a bit:

> God declared: *"Let there be light!"* (Gen 1:3) And light, travelling at 186,000 miles a second, exploded from His mouth (for *"God is light"*, 1 John 1:5) forever separating the night from the day!

That is the power of words and in making declarations.

And, it is in reference to this great creative power of God that the Apostle Paul in Romans 1:20 (King James Version) wrote:

> *"For the invisible things of Him from the creation of the world are clearly seen, being understood by the* **things that are made***, even His eternal power and Godhead; so that they are without excuse".*

In this verse, Paul used the Greek word *"poiema"* from which *"things that are made"* was translated.

"Poiema" is used only one other time in the New Testament. This time to refer to God's re-creative power wherein humankind is recreated as God's "workmanship" as described again by Paul in Ephesians 2:10 (King James Version):

> *"For we are His* **workmanship***, created in Christ Jesus unto good works, which God hath before ordained that we should walk in them."*

The word "workmanship" is also translated from *"poiema"*.

Now, this is the point I find most exciting—the English word "poem" is derived from *"poiema"*. Wow! So, not only am I a part of God's first poetic expression, creation, but I am born again or recreated in Jesus unto good works as God's poem, His work of art, His masterpiece.

In the two greatest demonstration of His creative power, the creation of the universe and recreation or redemption of humankind, God describes Himself as Poet! **God is the consummate and unparalleled poet**.

According to Willis Barnstone, He *". . . is the great invisible poet of the world. Like the Old Testament prophets, He communicates in wisdom poetry—in short maxims, in narrative parable, and always in memorable metaphor"*. It is only fitting then, that the renewed me, as God's greatest poetic masterpiece, is reflected through poems.

The poetic expression of Jesus resonates throughout all time as a reminder to humankind of the depth of the Father's love for us:

> *"Look at the lilies in the field and how they grow they don't*
> *work or make their clothing yet Solomon in all his glory was*
> *not dressed as beautifully as they are. And if God cares so*
> *wonderfully for wildflowers that are here today and thrown into*
> *the fire tomorrow He will certainly care for you"*.
> (Saint Matthew 6:28-30, Life Application Study Bible)

My desire for you is that you will not only read my poetic expressions; but that you will also hear the poetic voice of Jesus and will concur with me in saying: *"of all that He's created, I am God's workmanship, His poem"*.

HIS WORKMANSHIP . . . GOD'S POEM

19 November 2008

Conceived in movements of rhyme

Birthed through rhythmic pulsing of heart

Developed in plots weighed and measured

Composed in stanzas framed by challenges and victories

Punctuated by expressions of supplications

Expressed in lyric of uninhibited praise

Resolutely recited in the everlasting now

Recreated in idioms of surrender

Foreshadowed in knowing and being known

Understood in elocution of clarity distinct

Evolved through spiritual healing

Climaxed in all that He's created

His workmanship

God's poem

Before Word—Part II

Why moments? It is principally for this reason—I am learning to pay attention to the "moments" of life rather than contemplating life in its entirety. Prior to this way of being, I would focus on the totality of life which at one point literally stopped me in my tracks as I became overwhelmed by the enormity and felt like life was but a routine of meaninglessness.

Herein came the reality check:
The meaning of life is life itself!

So I came to the realization that life is but a collection of **MOMENTS**—snippets of time compounded in minutes . . . hours . . . days . . . weeks . . . months . . . years. And, these moments are meaningless until defined by me.

It is only as I embarked on this journey to understand and know the heart of God that I began learning to define and live in the moments of life. Learning that amidst the many tasks and duties, the laughter and the tears, the ups and downs, the failures and successes, the losses and gains, the blessings and misfortunes—life happens. And also learning that it is in maximizing the moments, which over time will be the sum-total of my days/my years/my life that I will truly live. I can choose to complain, be stressed and overwhelmed or I can choose to live positively in the moment. So can you.

To *"live in the moment"* means to be PRESENT in your life. Or, in other words, to be cognizant of what's going on around you in that moment and to be appreciative of the experience for just what it is. In that moment, do not be bogged down with thoughts of what was, what could have been or what will be, but be focused on what IS.

To *"live in the moment"* also means to live in the NOW. Nigerian musician Babatunde Olatunji understood this "live-in-the-moment" way of being when he said: *"Yesterday is history. Tomorrow is a mystery. And today? Today is a gift. That's why we call it the present."* I've seen Babatunde's quote taken a step further and paraphrased as: *"NOW is a gift, that's why it's called the PRESENT".*

NOW is pregnant with possibilities.
NOW can be anything and everything!

The past on the other hand is just that, the past. There is nothing you can do to change it though you may be able to make amends for actions taken that caused yourself or others hurt and to forgive and seek forgiveness. The only merit attributed to the past should be as a point of reference, not a place of residence.

I will be the first to admit that living a moment-by-moment life is not easy but it is possible, as are all things, with God. It is He who said, *"If ye shall ask anything in My name, I will do it"* (Saint John 14:14, King James Version). And anything means . . . well, ANYTHING!

And when we fall into old patterns of living-in-the-past-and-being-anxious-about-tomorrow, it is God who also admonished us to live like the birds. Here's a poetic rendition of Jesus:

> *"Look at the birds of the air*
> *For they neither sow nor reap*
> *Nor gather into barns*
> *Yet their heavenly Father feeds them*
> *Are you not of more value than they?"*
> (Saint Matthew 6:26, New King James Version)

Basically Jesus is admonishing us to live as birds do. This does not mean we are not to make plans for our livelihood, but rather that our lives should be guided by the knowledge that even when we make plans we should be open to being directed by God's purpose. For *"a man's heart plans his way, but the Lord directs his steps"*; and, *"there are many plans in a man's heart, nevertheless the Lord's counsel that will stand".* (Proverbs 16:9; 19:21 New King James Version)

Jesus' invitation is for us to trust our Heavenly Father and in so doing not be consumed with worries about tomorrow but instead to unwrap our PRESENT, embrace each NOW for what it is, and live fully in that MOMENT like the next one will not come.

Christian revolutionary, Leo Tolstoy said it beautifully when he wrote: *"There is only one time that is important—NOW! It is the most important time because it is the only time that we have any power".*

Subsequently, if it is as I argue—that life is but a collection of **MOMENTS**—what is death then but the breath of life evaporated in a flash . . . an instant . . . a jiffy . . . ?

At the cessation of your **MOMENTS** *"when death finds you, hope that it finds you alive".* (Japanese proverb)

failures ups   fears leading
forgiveness   restoration
empathy realization   hope   magical
satisfaction   laughter courage faith

MOMENTS

receiving encouragement
downs expectation joy patience familial
change truthfulness tears reflection
actualization merriment
losses teachable learning giving peace
healing following blessings
bouncebackability
anticipation
miraculous
justice
love

Dear Reader,

Scatter words in the space below to describe the various MOMENTS you have experienced:

Nevertheless, Afterward

My Heart-Poem to God

Dear God

I come to You with a heart filled with gratitude and thanksgiving. Thank You for channeling in me a bit of Your poetic-artistic creativity. Without the art You embedded in each nook and cranny of creation, the earth and all that dwell here would just be bland because truly the "earth" without the "art" that is You is just "eh". Thank You for the art unfolded in majestic mountains, breathtaking meadows, massive oceans, boundless skies and splendiferous birds, flowers and faunas.

Father, every creative insight and every word that was stringed together to form each poem in this book was an offspring of Your creativity. Thank You for helping me to conceive this work of art and I pray that as it is read it will find the path to hearts and lead them to the source of all creativity and all art—You the consummate poet, the ultimate restorer and only Savior in whom they will mature and grow.

I thank You also for the each moment You have gifted me since birth. I never want to take it for granted that life is a guarantee. Please help me to always be appreciative of each moment and truly live in the gift that is "now".

With all my love and devotion
Your daughter
Dee

Your Heart-Poem to God

Dear Reader,

As you reflect on the various moments of your life, write below the sentiments of your heart to God as you would to a friend. Be free to truly express your feelings be it of appreciation, gratitude, fear, anger etc. and be open to the response from God's heart to yours.

❦

You are now embarking on this moment-by-moment journey, each poem an insight into an encounter with the Divine!

❦

CHAPTER 1

FAMILIAL MOMENTS

We each experience familial moments—moments with our family wherein we experience the full range of emotions, from love to rage and every feeling in between; and moments articulated in laughing and crying and all other expressions in between.

Our feelings about our families are as varied as we each are distinct one from the other, none of us having the same fingerprint. Yet, there is one thing we all have in common—we had no choice in being born or the families we were born into. That is our bloodline-family. Although we had no choice in our bloodline families, we were assigned to our families by God's design.

Then there are families of choice. People who are not connected by bloodline-kinship but whose choice to love and care for each other formed psychological– and spiritual-kinships that is as sacred and, in some cases, even stronger and more wholesome than bloodline-kinships.

Enter now on the path to **Familial Moments!**

Before Word

"And I will add unto thy days fifteen years; and I will deliver thee and this city out of the hand of the king of Assyria; and I will defend this city for mine own sake, and for my servant David's sake". (2 Kings 20:6, King James Version)

*C*he verse above pertains to Hezekiah, King David's great-great-great-great-great-great-great-great-great-great-great-great grandson. By the time Hezekiah assumed the throne as King, thirteen Kings had already reigned for a period of two hundred and ninety-four years. In other words, David was dead for almost three hundred years. However, when Hezekiah was sick unto death and the Assyrian army was about to invade his kingdom, he prayed to God for good health and deliverance. God responded by adding fifteen additional healthy years to Hezekiah and gave him victory over the invading forces.

What resonated with me when I read this verse was God's emphasis that He acted for David's sake. This is absolutely amazing! You may not see immediately why I find this fascinating so let me paint a picture of how my imagination envisioned what transpired when I read this text.

The prophet had just delivered the news to Hezekiah that he was about to die and departed from the bedroom of the King. Hezekiah immediately falls prostrate at his bedside beseeching God for healing and deliverance. His prayer is one of millions ascending to the throne of God, but when Hezekiah's prayer reached God's ears it immediately triggered the memory of God who recalled David. He recalled a man whose heart resembled His; a man who worshipped Him with such reckless abandon and intensity that there was leftover worship, praise, love and adoration. And immediately God pulled down on David's blessings stored up for almost three hundred years and credited it to his offspring removed by twelve generations. So instant was the response, it came between the time the prophet left

Hezekiah and reached the courtyard. God instructed him to return to Hezekiah with the counter message of good health and deliverance.

This ability to call down credit from blessings stored up in heaven by an ancestor is as relevant to my mother and me as they were for David and Hezekiah. You see, long before I knew how to pray I had a prayer-warrior interceding on my behalf storing up blessings in heavenly places that when needed, I could redeem by claiming: *"for the sake of Agnes, Your servant"*.

There are many ways to describe my mother—Agnes Elizabeth Burke—but none is more apt than to say my mother is a Christian. Not only did she teach me the ways of Christ, but she lived them. And, even when I migrated to live with my father I did not forsake her teachings; when I walked they led me, when I laid down they watched over me, and when I was awake they talked with me. She raised me in the theology of Jesus Christ.

The building blocks and steppingstones along the path of my life have been carved and laid-out by the sacrifices my mother made so that both the interior and exterior of my foundation are long-lasting and resilient.

There is nothing that I can ever do to repay my mother—not that she would want me to—but I live my life as a tribute to her. Even though I'm all grown up and have lived away from my mom since my teenage years, my actions are still motivated by *"what would mommy think"* because I never want to disappoint her or cause her hurt.

This piece, ***"Mother's Tribute"*** was written for my mom, **Agnes Elizabeth Burke**, on her birthday in 1997.

Dawn A. Minott

MOTHER'S TRIBUTE

9 February 1997

You carried me beneath your heart
Cared for me from the very start

Cradled safely in your arms
Protected from growing-up storms

All I've accomplished and all that I am
Is because you taught me how to stand

Firm and strong, you laid a foundation
Of high morals and self-determination

Sacrificed yourself so I was defined
Gave up your dreams to nurture mine

Instilled in me the will to believe
That I can be all I wanted to achieve

So to you, Mother, this tribute I convey
No gifts or words can fully say

Me—all that I am and all I will do
My life, dear Mom, is my tribute to you

Before Word

𝐴 significant part of my formative years were spent with one of my maternal aunts. This is not peculiar to Jamaican society since, like in many parts of the world, extended families play substantial roles in child caring and childrearing. This experience shaped my life-course in fundamental ways.

First, I learned early that my care and sustenance were not contingent solely on my mother, but that she belonged to and could access the resources of a wide family network and support system and therefore so could I. That network included my aunt who raised me as if I was her child so much so people assumed she was my mother. I knew I was loved and I also learned how to discern and receive love. This attribute served me well later in life as I've lived in different countries and needed this perceptive ability to form healthy relationships and to tap into support systems while away from my family.

Second, I learned early to assimilate quickly to new and different situations and living locales. At the time I was sent to live with my aunt, she resided in Kingston while my mom lived in the parish of Saint Andrew. Kingston is the capital of Jamaica and geographically it is not far from Saint Andrew (as you'll see on the map). So, in terms of geographical location and travel time, I was not very far away from my mom. However, as a child, it felt like another world; not only because

my young mind could not adequately comprehend the true distance, but also because Jamaicans typically refer to those living outside of Kingston as living in "the country", meaning in the rural areas, and this denotes a far distance from someone living in Kingston, or "in town". So, in my childhood mind my mother living in "the country" while I was living with my aunt "in town" was translated to my mom being as far away from me as north is from south. I missed my mom immensely but I learned the knack of assimilating to new living environments. This ability placed me in good stead for a career as an International Civil Servant with the United Nations, which requires regular rotation from one duty station to another.

Later when I asked my mom why I was sent to live with my aunt, she explained it was to give me greater access to the resources my aunt could provide for me in Kingston such as schooling. She could not have made a better choice of an "other mother" for me.

In addition to loving me as if I was her child and providing for my daily sustenance and care, my aunt nurtured me. She was strict but fair. Proper decorum was expected of me at all times and in all situations regardless of how my friends behaved. I remember once it was rumoured that I did something wrong, it was truly a rumour, I was innocent; but my aunt's scolding was along the lines of: *"if you're right, you're wrong; and if you're wrong, you're double-wrong so don't get your name called in anything"*. From this type of discipline I learned to choose my friends carefully, to be a leader and not to succumb to negative peer pressure.

My aunt had an unusual, but effective way of reeling me in if I was stepping out of line. She used her eyes! She had a stare for each misstep and even ones to scold. I quickly learned the stare which said, *"if you don't stop right now, you're gonna get it"* to prevent any form of punishment. It was effective because I was fearful of being hit and avoided every occasion that could cause me embarrassment. The silent-intense stare kept me in line so I walked the "straight and narrow" and escaped the disciplining rod.

Like my mom, my aunt nurtured me in the ways of God. And true to her commitment as a "career student" and a teacher, she ensured I stayed the course in my scholastic endeavours.

The generosity of my aunt, affectionately called Aunty Cherry, and her commitment to my overall development is embodied in the piece *"Other Mother"*.

Aunty Cherry was the first to teach me the acrostic style of writing. It's only fitting, then, that this piece is acrostically written in dedication to my aunt, **Olga Henrietta Simmons**.

Dawn A. Minott

OTHER MOTHER

12 February 2011

Other Mother

Lovingly

Giving

Accepting the

Heavenly call to be a mom before you birthed a child

Ever loving, always caring, giving from a heart that's kind

Nurturing in all your ways, provider, educator, guide

Rigorous in disciplining, keeping wayward feet in stride

Ingeniously redirecting with the *"behave or else"* stare

Effortlessly correcting behaviour without a strap or fear

Teacher is who you are it's what you've been to me

Tapping into the potential the wellspring of who I'd be

Always grateful I will be, Aunt Cherry, Other Mother to me

Before Word

*O*ver the years, the structure and definition of "family" has changed. And, because of sin, families are flawed so that the worst kind of abuse sometimes happens within families.

In my case, I grew up with only my mother before I lived with my aunt and her husband. My situation is not unique in that the number of female-headed homes is spiralling upward and the trend does not appear to be reversing. However, this was not God's original blueprint. He intended for children to be parented by both mother and father. In fact, in addressing the rearing of children, fathers are specifically called upon by God to bring up their children and to do so in the discipline and instruction of the Lord. (Ephesians 6:4)

Without fathers raring their children, how do boys learn to be men and how do girls learn about men when they are being "fathered" by mothers? Upon what standard do children who have been abandoned by their fathers formulate their concepts of a father's attributes?

As a child who grew up without my father, both *"Defector"* and *"God Blesses the Child Who Hurts"* were written from that experience.

The word "defector" is used to define someone who disowns allegiance to his or her country and takes up residence in another. On November 18th, 1996 when *"Defector"* was penned, it emanated from the deep recesses of my mind. I had reflected on my earliest memories and was confronted with the reality of what I always knew but had not voiced—"something" was missing from my family source. The impact my father's absence had on my formative years was telling; he had indeed defected from my life, he had disowned his allegiance to me and had taken up residence somewhere else. The "something" missing was the presence of my father. *"Defector"* was written from my experience and that of others with absentee fathers.

Though I later had to the opportunity to meet and then live with my father, as you will see in the piece *"God Blesses the Child Who Hurts,"* our relationship, though mended, has visible signs of cracks and the remnants of repair.

Both pieces, *"God Blesses the Child Who Hurts"* and *"Defector"*, were written as part of accepting and valuing the relationship with my father for what it is, forgiving, letting go of the past and beginning the process of restoration and healing.

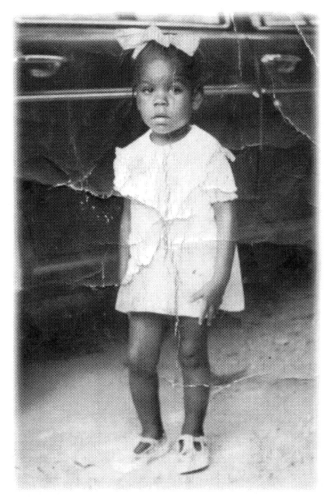

Dawn A. Minott, 2 years old

DEFECTOR

18 November 1996

She must have been two, or was it three or four?
A small intuitive child, zealous to know more
Trying to figure out what's different on her own
Wondering always what's missing from home

Where were you when your child was born
In the wee-early hours of that fateful Tuesday morn?
Did you care if your child were a girl or boy?
Did the birth make you elated with joy?
What of your promise to return one day
To the mother of your child who had to stay?

Did you wonder if it were a boy, if he'd grow up to be like you
Ditching his paternal rights and his responsibilities too?
Or if he'd realize there ain't nothing wrong
For a woman to have a man who stays strong?

And, if it were a girl, did she grow up to resent?
Or was she confident, did she represent
The strength of the woman with whom she grew
Who gave up her dreams so her child's may come true?

Your son grew up, learned how to be a man
Best teacher he had was a woman
Your daughter filled a void your absence left there
She relied on a woman who knew how to care

A woman who sacrificed her life for her child, your child
While all the time never seeming to mind
Young boys growing up, no fathers to emulate
Young girls choosing men like you, imitate

You left behind a woman to father your child
A community of men running wild
Parenting is a role intended for two
Don't leave it all to the mother she did not make the rule

GOD BLESSES THE CHILD WHO HURTS

12 May 1997

From experiences encountered each passing day
I grow, just a little more
Now I know, I'm never really fully grown
In my heart, buried deep within
A child yearns to be known, to be loved, to grow

It must have been me
I was not what he wanted
Did I cry too loudly?
Did I make him mad?
Did I bring him laughter?
No!
He must have been sad
There's no other explanation
He'd just simply gone away
Never held me as a baby
Never fed me as a child
Never called me his little girl
Never owned me as his child

Growing up I felt abandoned
Kept it hidden, deep down inside
Didn't want to let her know
Didn't want to make her sad
For he had left her behind too
Cried when I knew she could not hear me
Faked smiles to make her glad
Created an image of him
One embedded in my mind
One that would never ever leave me
One that loved me, kept me sane

Then that image, it got shattered
Reality came crashing in
Tearing away what I had dreamed of
Leaving me bare
Scared again

Said he loved me, but he hurt me
Said he'd protect me, but put me out
Said he'd always be there for me
Now I'm living all alone
Ate my food from people's handout
Slept in other people's bed
Love earned a new meaning then—
Hurt me, abandon me, leave me all alone again

Tried to mend the broken fences
Three times
Rejected o'er again
Sending letters
Making phone calls
He just didn't want to be there
He simply didn't care

Time to move on from the hurt now
Time to count it all but loss
Time to heal my broken spirit
Time to find the child who's lost

Now the child within has grown up
Life had dealt some hurtful blows
No more misled childhood fantasies
No more hoping it would be so
I would never be his "little girl"

I am so much stronger now
Strength from the ultimate source above
Yes, I've had some days of sorrow
Days when only tears would do
Days when living hurt so deeply
But the alternative too scary to do
Days when I could see no rainbows
Only stormy clouds and rain

But Mom—yes Mom!
She had laid a firm foundation
Now I'll build on it and grow
He will never be my "daddy dearest"
I've accepted
It's time to let it go

Even though I couldn't see it
God was always by my side
So to those who come behind me
Confused, abused, used
God can mend the broken pieces
Find your child who lives within

Listen
God has shown me
Pick yourself up
Start again
Experience new birth
And, know this
God blesses the child who hurts

Before Word

 n growing up without my father, the impact of paternal absence influenced very strongly my views of "father", and I later realized this also included my view of God as Father.

As a child, I had transferred and attached my feelings about and impressions of my father—truant, unreliable, untrustworthy—to my concept of God as Father. And, even more debilitating were the fears that bred out of these feelings: the fear of being abandoned and of being rejected. Journeying to the heart of God for someone like me, whose insights into the heart of God as my Father was obscured by these feelings and fears, was tumultuous.

At some point on the journey, I somehow got it fixed in my mind that if I were good enough to work my way into God's heart, only then would He love me. So, I stopped listening to secular music, I read only spiritual books, I prayed every day, I attended church faithfully, I didn't go clubbing, didn't drink alcohol or smoke. In and of themselves these things are good but my intentions were not. You see, I wanted to "work" my way into God's heart. But, the harder I trekked up this mountain of self-righteousness the farther my fall to the valley of despair would be, placing me further away from the very place I craved the most, the heart of God.

I could not comprehend how God as Father could love me just because . . . , for no other reason than that He just loves me and loves me unconditionally. I could not comprehend that He would not reject me or abandon me especially when He could see the real me, for no matter how hard I tried to make myself into what I believe would make Him love me and not leave me, the more unlike Him I became.

The truth of the matter was simply this: I could not understand why God/Father would love me unconditionally because I did not believe my father loved me. I could not understand why God/Father would stay and would accept me because my father did not.

So there I was living alone, taking care of myself and meeting all of my needs when God did the most amazing thing—He placed me in the lives of a beautiful, caring and loving couple, **Edna** and **Wilbert Minnifee**—materializing His promise to place the solitary into families (Psalm 68:6). And, for the first time I called a man "daddy" because he was indeed "daddy" to me. It is in this act of giving me an earthly dad that God won my daughterly affections.

I use this opportunity to express my heart-felt love and appreciation to **Edna** and **Wilbert Minnifee.** It was only after God repositioned my opinion of "father" through my earthly "daddy" that I could find my place in His heart and accept Him as my Abba, my Daddy, again making real another of His promises—that He'd be a father to the fatherless (Psalm 68:5).

However, I got the idea for the title of the upcoming poem while living in South Africa, when after having me share my experiences of growing up without a father to a few gatherings my aunty-friend, **Gail Masondo**, challenged me to start a "daddy's girl ministry".

After all I've been through and to have come out on the other side of it all as blessed as I am and not bitter or emotionally damaged, is nothing short of a miracle.

The upcoming piece was written from this assurance—I know that I know that God loves me, and I also know that He FAVORS me and I'm His girl. I Am *"Daddy's Girl".*

DADDY'S GIRL

13 November 2011

if I Took Off The Mask
fully Unveiled Me
opened Up My Heart
revealed The Real Me
the Me No One Else Sees
could You Really Love Me?
love Me Just As I Am
UNCONDITIONALLY?

if I Let Go Off Of The Hurt
frailty From The Brokenness Within
trusted You With All Of Me
loosened My Grasp
letting Go And Letting You
would You Really Love Me?
love Me Just As I Am
UNCONDITIONALLY?

i'm Scared, Deathly Afraid, Unsure
but I Don't Want This Pain No More
if I Surrendered
gave Up What Has Sustained Me
turned My Care Over To You
could You Really Accept Me?
accept Me Just As I Am
UNCONDITIONALLY?

the Fear Of Being Rejected
that You Too Would Refuse Me
constrained Me
kept Me From Receiving Your Love
now That I'm Reaching For Your Embrace
would You Really Accept Me?
accept Me Just As I Am
UNCONDITIONALLY?

now It Feels That You Console Me
cradling Me Upon Your Lap
nestling My Head Upon Your Chest
with Each Heartbeat Reverberating
"I Love You, You're My Girl"

strong Yet Gentle Arms Encircling
all My Doubts And Fears Erasing
confident Am I In Knowing
I AM LOVED, ACCEPTED, WANTED—
UNCONDITIONALLY

Always will I need You
Never will I stray from You
Thankful You will stay
Not turn away, forsake me
Grateful You are slow to anger
You find delight in being gracious
Satisfied in knowing You're a Father to the fatherless
Fulfilled in accepting You call me Your beloved
Content in receiving a new name, You surnamed me
Comfortable in acknowledging

I am
DADDY'S GIRL

Nevertheless, Afterward

My Heart-Poem to God

Dear Abba,

*You called me by Your name, **surnamed** me even before I knew You*.*

I am so grateful that not only did You give me a new name, You gave me Your surname, the family name—the name You passed down from generation to generation—which identifies me as daughter and a heir to all that You are and all that You have. Thank You for the confidence borne from my new name. Thank You for loving me so completely.

Thank You for my family—my mother, father, brothers, sisters, nieces, nephews, aunts, uncles and cousins—all of whom have been the spokes in my support system.

Thank You for being the repairer of the breach and the mender of broken relationships.

I love You Abba! Thank You for loving me.

Always Your girl
Gratefully,
Dee

*(Isaiah 45:4, King James Version)

Your Heart-Poem to God

Dear Reader,

If you've also grown up without your father or mother, or if the relationship with either parent is not as you desire it, and if the opportunity to talk with your dad or mom still exists, I pray you will be motivated in this moment to make the call and make amends.

Use the space below to write your heart-poem to God—you may ask Him to empower you and to make your father or mother receptive to receive your call or visit.

CHAPTER 2

MOMENTS OF SELF-DISCOVERY

Self-discovery can be understood as the act or process of achieving understanding or knowledge of oneself.

For me, the journey of self-discovery started through the process of keeping a daily journal.

I got my first journal soon after moving to Canada to live with my father. For all intents and purposes he was a stranger as were his wife and son; and of course so were the neighbours and the students at school. Even the weather was foreign to me. I arrived in Canada on a very cold January day, and when I exited the airport there was snow piled high! So, from home to school to family to schoolmates to weather, I was lost in a world that was completely different from the one I grew up in.

With no one to talk to—to share my deepest thoughts, my fears, my longings, my hopes and desires—I started journaling. Some journal entries turned into poems and opened this creative outlet. The act of journaling changed my life; it was a tool that helped me to understand who I was and who I was becoming.

Enter now on the path to **Moments of Self-Discovery!**

Before Word

*O*f all the hostilities the devil exerts against the children of God, he specializes in psychological warfare—messing with our minds through the spirit of fear, doubt, guilt, worry, anger etc. But, the most powerful weapon in his arsenal is that of low self-esteem. For many years he skillfully wielded this weapon against me and every time he swung, it connected and I succumbed to a barrage of self-deprecating responses:

> *I'm too tall!* *I'm not smart enough!*
> *I'm not worthy!* *I'm too skinny!*
> *I'm not deserving!* *I'm not pretty enough!*

Even as a Christian, I had a low self-concept. I know I'm not alone for many Christians, in spite of the myriad assurances in the Word of God of who we are in Him, are shackled with the feelings of inferiority and inadequacy and of thinking we are not worthy enough. But, as I'm journeying to the heart of God I'm learning that as long as I keep my focus on self, independent of what and who God says I am, I will remain immobilized, paralyzed and inept to reach my full potential.

Along the path of refocusing, I have found many reminders in the Word of God that have resonated with my spirit and have built me up to live in the reality that I'm Daddy's girl, an heir to the Kingdom of God. In Romans 8:17 Paul states: *"And if children, then heirs; heirs of God, and joint-heirs with Christ . . ."* (King James Version) Now I live boldly in the knowledge that I am worthy; that I'm enough; and, that I am perfect and whole just as I am. And, so are you!

Remember, you are a one-of-a-kind edition. You were purposefully designed and masterfully created. God says:

> *"I am your Creator. You were in My care even before you were born . . . . Don't be terrified! You are My chosen servant,*

My very favorite". (Isaiah 44:2, Contemporary English Version)

Remember, you were created by design. Before you were born, there was a blueprint—a master plan—laying out the days of your life in advance. There was a rendering of everything about you including the exact timing of your birth, how long you would live, where you would live, and the color of your skin. God says:

> *"From one man He made every nation of men that they should inhabit the whole earth; and He determined the times set for them and the exact places where they should live."* (Acts 17:26, New International Version)

Remember, you are intimately known. Even before you were conceived, God knew everything about who you are and what you are capable of doing. He says:

> *"Nothing about [you] is hidden from [Me]! [You] were secretly woven together . . . , with [My] own eyes [I] saw [your] body being formed. Even before [you were] born, [I] had written in [My] book everything [you] would do."* (Psalm 139:15-16, Contemporary English Version)

Remember, you were planned for. God left no detail of your existence to chance. Even if your parents did not plan to conceive you, you are not an accident. God planned for you to be here. In fact, He made a plan long before you were born to adopt you into His family. This is what He says:

> *"Long before [I] laid down earth's foundations, [I] had [you] in mind, had settled on [you] as the focus of [My] love. Long, long ago [I] decided to adopt [you] into [My] family"* (Ephesians 1:4-5, The Message Bible)

And, most importantly, **don't forget to remember, God thinks the world of you!** He has a **SO-LOVE** for you:

"For God SO loved [you], that He gave His only begotten Son, that whosoever believeth in Him should not perish, but have everlasting life." (Saint John 3:16 King James Version)

And should you ever forget, God beseeches you:

"Listen to me", He pleads, *"You whom I have upheld since your birth, and have carried since you were born. Even to your old age and gray hairs I am He, I am He who will sustain you. I have made you and I will carry you; I will sustain you . . . ."* (Isaiah 46:3-4, Today's New International Version)

You are God's masterpiece, His poetry, His ***"One-of-a-Kind Edition"***.

ONE-OF-A-KIND EDITION

14 April 2011

Before you were conceived God chose
The womb of your safekeeping
The date and time of your birth
The purpose for your attributes
The distinctiveness of your identity
The level of your intellect
The contours of your face
The shape of your body

In all the world
There is no one else like you
You're unique—one else possesses your traits
You're peculiar—no one else thinks the way you do
You're distinctive—no one acts in the same way you do
You're matchless—no one else has lived your experiences
You're nonpareil—birthed for such a time and place as this
You're incomparable—designed for a purpose only you can fulfill
You're unequalled—no one can do what you do the way you do it

You're onomatopoetic—free to be who you are like waterfall
cascading
You're delineated by moments—brief intervals of time
compounded in
. . . minutes
. . . hours
. . . days
. . . weeks
. . . months
. . . years
To fashion a one-of-a kind edition
The sui generis
You

Before Word

*O*ne of the things my friends know about me is that I love celebrating my birthday. This wasn't always the case. In growing up, my birthdays passed as any other day; there was nothing special, no celebration. However, as part of my quest in learning how to bask in the moments I have been privileged with, I discovered a love in commemorating the day of my birth.

There was a time in my life when I was so busy trying to survive, milestones were simply checked off as I barreled forward to accomplish the next thing on my life-list, and tried to keep myself from drowning under the responsibilities of caring for others and myself. During this time, the old adage *"stop and smell the roses"* meant nothing to me. Stop and smell the roses? Not when there were classes to attend, courses to ace, students to teach, research to do, money to earn, food and clothes and books to purchase, tuition and rent to pay, aid to extend to others and sanity to maintain. I was so busy surviving, I was not living.

This 'rat race' continued until September 2003 when I found myself at the intersection of peace-of-mind and wit's-end crossroads. There I was standing at peace-of-mind corner contented that:

- ✓ I had finished University at the top of my class with a BA, MA and a specialized Certificate. Check!
- ✓ I had landed my 'dream job' with the United Nations right out of University. Check!
- ✓ I was back in the Caribbean working in the beautiful, picturesque island of Barbados. Check!
- ✓ I was doing the thing I loved the most, travelling. Check!
- ✓ I was engaged to be married. Check!

My life was running like clockwork. I had followed the routine, put in the hard work and the results came. However, through all of these accomplishments not only had I neglected to give God full credit, I had not stopped once—not once—to appreciate,

42

acknowledge or celebrate the accomplishments. I had simply checked them off the list. I had the trappings of success, but was unfulfilled. I had survived, but I had not lived.

That's where I was at the other side of the intersection—wit's-end corner—exhausted, exasperated and out of moves to run my life. In desperation I cried out for help. In that state of helplessness and full surrender I heard God's voice, strong yet gentle, directing me to trust Him completely and to be grateful.

Now:

- ✓ I stop and smell the roses, literally! (Every week, except for unforeseen circumstances, I purchase roses to remind me to stop and appreciate the gift that is life.) Check!
- ✓ If there is a word to be said, I'll say it now (I do this in affirming the people in my life—*"I love you"*, *"I appreciate you"*, *"I admire you"*—nothing is left unsaid). Check!
- ✓ If there is a trip to take, I'll take it now. (My ultimate dream trip was to Africa. The day I landed on the continent only the fear of being taken straight from the airport ramp to the asylum prevented me from kissing the ground, that's how appreciative I was). Check!
- ✓ If there is a symphony to enjoy, a play to see, a concert to sing along with or a production to take pleasure in, I'll do it all now. (I've collected and stowed in my *"I Did It!"* basket a plethora of ticket stubs and programs from events attended and postcards from countries visited.) Check!
- ✓ And, I celebrate my birthday. But because this is my ultimate-most-favorite moment, I don't just celebrate birthday, I celebrate "birth-month". Check!

I see my birthday as a memorial to the time when the Almighty stopped all the God-things He does—you know, like keeping planets from colliding, the earth rotating on its perfect orbit around the sun, 7 billion-plus human beings breathing, flowers blooming, and telling oceans *"thus far you may come, but no farther, and here your proud waves must stop"* (Job 38:11)—just long enough for me.

My birthday commemorates
MY moment in time.

God could have birthed me on any other day, but He chose a Tuesday, exactly two weeks into the fourth month of the year (April 14th). I imagine on that early Tuesday morning (I was born at dawn), God commissioned my guardian angel saying: *"Today, I'm birthing My precious daughter, Dawn Angela. She is your charge; ensure she arrives back to Me safely".*

And my Guardian Angel has been with me ever since. On the day when s/he sits down with me and our Father, I can only imagine her/his stories will be regaled with all those "but God . . . moments". You know, those moments when I was "dead" in trespasses and sins; when my behavior was governed by the lusts of the flesh and the perversion of my mind as I walked according to my sin-nature going contrary to the will of God. Yet, in each of those moments I was spared from the consequences because of the Bible's two most powerful words strung together: "But God" (Ephesians 2:4).

I can't wait to hear how my Guardian Angel recalls those "But God . . ." moments. But, until then, I've composed my rendition of **"BUT GOD . . ."** as a tribute of thanksgiving to my Guardian Angel. It was written to commemorate birth-months past and to be thankful, in advance, for birth-months to come.

BUT GOD . . .

14 April 2011

I could have been sick, laid up in a hospital bed . . .
I could have been dead, buried six feet below . . .
I could have been mourning the untimely loss of loved ones . . .
I could have been without a job, destitute and poor . . .
I could have been homeless, sleeping in the streets . . .
I could have been depressed, even lost my mind . . .
I could have no love, no friends, no family to call my own . . .
I could have been burdened by sin, lost without hope . . .

BUT GOD

He's been my Sustainer, my Provider, my Stronghold
No need He hasn't supplied
He's even met some wants

He's been my Director, my Compass, my Guide
No plans of the enemy He hasn't thwarted
And measured those He's allowed

He's been my Confidante, my Father, my Best-Friend
No prayers He hasn't answered
His "no" and "wait-awhile" were gentle, His "yeses" blow my mind

He's been my every thing
Where would I be if it hadn't been for
BUT GOD

Before Word

*A*s I'm on this journey to the heart of God, the greatest compliment anyone can give me is to say: *"I'm Christ-like".*

A few years ago one of the NBA's greatest players sparked a barrage of commercials and made popular the slogan: *"I wanna be like Mike".* Yes, he was the tongue-extending-leg-kicking-hanging-in-midair-dunk machine. Every little boy, and big boys too, and even girls dribbled up and down basketball courts shuffling balls between legs and over shoulders mimicking the gimmicks of Mike. Because of him, number 23 was the most popular jersey on and off the basketball court. And who can forget the lyrics of the popular jingle.

"I wanna be like Mike" ricocheted off tongues and echoed in the recesses of the hearts of millions of people all over the world who truly desired to be like Mike—Michael Jordon, that is.

But there is another Mike—Michael the Archangel, that is. He has been and will forever be the greatest. He has the most memorable marketing slogans of all time and through infinity:

JESUS LOVES YOU!

He desires to hear *"I wanna be like Christ!"* ricocheting off the tongues of all His children and see their lives like jerseys making popular His number, Saint John 3:16, so no one will forget the lyrics of the most popular declaration and promise:

> *"For God so loved the world that He gave*
> *His only begotten Son that whosoever believeth*
> *in Him should not perish but have*
> *everlasting life."*

The upcoming piece, *"I Wanna Be Like Christ!"*, is a challenge to parents—as your children are on the path of self-discovery, who are you encouraging them to be like? Christ?

Dawn A. Minott

I WANNA BE LIKE CHRIST!

26 May 2005

Kids at school act real cool
Dressed up in Gucci and Prada
Though they're my age
They're all decked out
Expensive things bling-blinging

Sometimes I want to fit in
Wear the latest style
But mom says she won't have it
I pout and frown, roll my eyes in disbelief
She's old-school, she just don't get it
I wanna act real cool
Hang with the popular crew
This church scene just ain't happening

Mom takes me aside, looks deep in my eyes
With love and compassion reminds me
You're the child of the King
A princess won't always fit in
The difference everyone will see

It's in the reverence in your stance when you bow to pray
The melody in your voice when you praise His name
It's the sincerity of your words when you speak the truth
It's the change they'll see when you're more like Him
You're growing up to be like Christ

That's right
I'm growing in Christ
I wanna be like Christ
Christ-like
A Christian girl, that's me

Now when I step in school
I walk as free as can be
'Cause no one's brand labels me
I know my true worth
There's faith in my step
Warmth in my smile
As I explain—

It's in the strength of my will
My dependence on Him
The grace of God fills my spirit
I've got purity of thought
His joy fills my heart
I'm covered by His blood
His righteousness directs me
I do what's pleasing in His sight
I'm growing up to be like Christ

That's right
I'm growing up in Christ
I wanna be like Christ
Christ-like
A Christian girl, that's me

Before Word

*C*he next poem was written in 1998 and at that time I made reference to videos and cassette tapes. In 2012, as I'm now preparing to publish this book, videos are now replaced by DVDs and Blu-Ray and cassette tapes replaced by CDs and iTunes.

A lot has changed in the world in the fourteen years since this piece was initially penned, not just in technological advancement, but also in all other spheres of life particularly on issues of morality and spirituality. However, far more has changed since Jesus walked this earth over 2,000 years ago.

In a moment of contemplation, I pondered what the process of self-discovery was like for Jesus. This led me into thoughts of how He would be if He lived on earth today, thoughts which influenced the poem, *"If Jesus Lived on Earth Today"*.

- Would Jesus use Twitter or Facebook to reach the masses?
- Would His "Sermon on the Mount" be the Sermon at Yankee or Wembley Stadium?
- Would He have a reality TV show, maybe called "Jesus Idol" or the "J-Factor"?
- Would He chase the exchangers of gossips and tattletales from His temple?
- Would He heal the blind, the lame and the depressed or would it be said, He did only a few miracles because of unbelief?

But, then, in the context of my own self-discovery, I reflected on what it would mean for me if Jesus—in His physical self—stopped by to visit me today? What would I do? Invite Him in? What would I say? *"Come on in. Take a seat. May I get you something to drink?"* Or would I be too astounded to speak? Maybe I'd just sit at his feet and wait for Him to speak. Wait! Would I even recognize Him? Of course I would? Would I? After all, He dwelt among humanity and many who studied the prophesies about Him, who witnessed His miracles and heard Him speak, still did not recognize Him for who He was. So, after all I've read about Him in the Bible, would I recognize Him?

What *"If Jesus Lived on Earth Today"*? In essence, He does in that He resides in hearts that are willing to receive Him. Hence, consistently asking myself "what if Jesus lived on earth today" should make me cognizant of the realness of His presence in my life and as such should inform the person I'm becoming as reflected in what I do, see and say.

Dawn A. Minott

IF JESUS LIVED ON EARTH TODAY

19 August 1998

If Jesus lived on earth today
The good news of salvation He'd always say
Or do you think He'd wait for a more opportune time,
Maybe when friends weren't around to be divine?

Would He always testify of His Father above?
Showing compassion, kindness and unconditional love?
Feeding the hungry and opening to the homeless a door?
Storing up treasures in heaven though on earth He'd be poor?

If Jesus lived on earth today
He would walk the straight and narrow all the way
Ignoring the broad way knowing that route
Would take Him farther away from the Truth

And if, unannounced, He knocked at your door,
Would He be in shock at all there was in store?
Would you have to hide the movies or change the songs you play?
Or would you bid Him welcome without a moment's delay?

If Jesus lived on earth today
Would He join the conversations in all you had to say?
Or would there be some *bleep . . . bleep . . . bleep . . .*
For those words you just couldn't complete?

Jesus does live on the earth today
He resides in hearts—mind what you do, see and say
He hears the temptations the adversary sends your way
He understands, He's been there, He wants to hear you say:
I can do all things through Christ who strengthens me,
For through His death, He's given me the victory

Before Word

ℐ often hear people say: *"I heard the voice of God"* or *"God said . . ."* and each time I hear that it increases my desire to also hear God's voice. However, on this journey to the heart of God I've learned that hearing the voice of God is not just an audible expression as Moses experienced, for example. What I have experienced is the voice of God through His written Word, the Holy Bible; or through the spoken word such as a sermon, a song, a devotional reading or conversations with friends.

One other way that I've heard the voice of God is by taking His promises as His direct pledge of commitment to me. This is what Abraham also did. He was strong in his faith in believing God's promise that he would have a son with Sarah. He was almost one hundred years old and Sarah's womb was dead but he did not stagger at the promise of God; rather, he was *". . . fully persuaded that what [God] had promised, He was also able to deliver".* (Romans 4:21, King James Version) In other words, God has the ability to back up every promise He makes with the requisite action.

Based on this assurance, when I have an issue I go to the Bible in search of a promise which speaks to the matter at hand, I insert my name in the promise, place my finger on the very promise and say to God: *"now do as you have said".* I discovered this practical way of engaging with God's word in one of my favorite devotional books, *"Streams in the Dessert";* but learned this boldness in "commanding" God, from the Psalmist David.

David, through the prophet Nathan had received many promises from God. However, on one occasion in wanting to see the word/ promise materialize, David said to God:

> *"Now, O Lord God, the word which You have spoken concerning Your servant, and concerning his house, establish it*

forever and **do as You have said***."* (2 Samuel 7:25 &
1 Chronicles 17:23, New King James Version)

It's like David was saying to God: *"put Your action where Your words
are"*. This was very bold of David, wouldn't you say?

By stating *"do as You have said"*, David was referring back to the
promises God had made him. This means, if I'm to be as bold I
must first know the promises of God. But not only must I know the
promises, I must know the God who made them. I must know that
what God promises, He does so on the basis of His **justness** and
holiness which will not permit Him to deceive me. I must know that
what God promises, He does so on the basis of His **graciousness**
and **goodness** which will not permit Him to forget. I must know that
what God promises, He does so on His inherent trait of **truth** which
will not permit Him to change. So when I say *"do as You have said"*, I
do so on the authority that whatever God promises He is bound by
and is able to make good on His word (Romans 4:21).

I've also learned that not only can I claim promises, but I can also
command God concerning His intentions for my life. He says:

*". . . . Ask Me of things to come concerning My [daughter
Dawn], and concerning the work of My hands command ye
Me".* (Isaiah 45:11, King James Version)

It is from this knowledge that *"**Just As He Promised**"* was
born.

JUST AS HE PROMISED

23 October 2007

Open my eyes that I may see You

Open my ears that I may hear You

Open my heart that I will love You

Open my intellect that I may know You

Open my understanding that I will trust You

Open my mind that I will be willing to be submitted to You

Open my soul so I'll be receptive to all You have ordained me to be

Then close me—all of me—in trusting that You will make good on
all Your promises to me

Nevertheless, Afterward

My Heart-Poem to God

Dearest Abba,

Thank You for enabling me to discover myself in who You say I am. When the enemy seeks to tell me otherwise Daddy, remind me that I am Your one-of-a-kind edition and that You created me for a purpose that only I can fulfill.

Thank You for allowing me successes and failures, happiness and sadness, ups and downs. Thank You for all my "times" and most of all for being with me through it all. Please help me to be like You in all I say and do.

Thanks for living in my heart, for Your promises which never fail and Your mercies that are given to me anew each morning.

From the deepest part of my heart, Abba, thank You!

I love You always,
Your daughter
Dee

Your Heart-Poem to God

Dear Reader

In the space below, share with God your journey of self-discovery.

ೞ

"Whatever you do, hold on to hope!
The tiniest thread will twist into an
unbreakable cord. Let hope anchor
you in the possibility that this is not the
end of your story, that change will
bring you to peaceful shores."

(Author Unknown)

ೞ

CHAPTER 3

My heart is home when I am:

loved
wanted
Cherished
honored
treasured
Respected
accepted
priviledged
Encouraged
protected

ENCOURAGED

My heart is home in You

Enter now on the path to **Moments of Encouragement!**

Before Word

℘ife has a way of derailing us, doesn't it?

For a while everything is going fine—things are good at school or on the job; things are good with your friends; things are good with your parents or with your children; bills are paid, you're in love; you're in good health—life is great!

And then, it seems like out of nowhere—coworkers and friends are at odds with you; children are acting up; parents just don't understand; you lose your job, can't pay your bills; loved ones die; your health is failing; and the love of your life is gone. And, just like that your life's season changes from summer-bliss to winter-misery. In these moments, be encouraged for:

> *"there is a time for everything, and a season for every activity under the heavens."* (Ecclesiastics 3:1, New International Version)

There is a time for ***"Seasons of the Soul"***.

SEASONS OF THE SOUL

14 March 1996

SUMMER comes with such splendour
All of creation shows its praise
Flowers bloom
Fruits ripen
Birds sing
All things experiencing rebirth
All things made anew
Summer's end ushers in

AUTUMN's colours
Golden red
Sunshiny yellow
Crispy brown
Leaves
Falling
Peacefully lying in a final resting place

WINTER's milky white, delicate snow flakes
Cascading
Falling
Covering all it reaches in fluffy softness

    SPRING's revitalizing rain
    Showering
    Washing
    Cleansing

Life is much like nature's seasons
Changing constantly and surely with the passing of time
We too must face life's passing seasons
Days of SUMMER's splendour
Obstacles faced
Challenges conquered
Goals surpassed

But as surely as
AUTUMN follows SUMMER
SPRING follows WINTER
We too must face our days of
SPRING-like rebirth
AUTUMN-like falling
SUMMER-like passion
WINTER-like coldness

We too are faced with the seasons
The seasons of the soul

Nevertheless, Afterward

My Heart-Poem to God

Dear Abba,

Today I pray from a Winter-like place in my heart. I pause to acknowledge what is—my heart is broken, I'm hurting. I am so grateful I can acknowledge this hurt in knowing that You have all my times in Your hands—my good times and my bad times. Take my heart and heal it and console me always in the knowledge that You will withhold no good thing from me. Abba, help me to trust You in believing that if I don't have it, it's not good and if it's good and I don't have it, it's on the way.

I am so grateful that what You say You will do and I will pass through this Winter-like season being stronger on the other side of Spring.

In the same way I thank You for the Summer-like experiences, I thank You for this Winter-like season too.

Always,
Your daughter
Dee

Your Heart-Poem to God

Dear Reader

You too are faced with seasons of the soul. Share with God your feelings in the season you're now experiencing. He's interested in hearing about all your experiences and emotions.

Before Word

"Do not be anxious about anything, but in everything, by prayer and petition, with thanksgiving, present your requests to God. And the peace of God, which transcends all understanding, will guard your hearts and your minds in Christ Jesus." (Philippians 4:6-7, New International Version)

I recall, it was very late the night of September 14th, 1993 when a friend called in despair. He was teetering on the edge of giving up, letting go; he thought life had dealt one too many blows.

Considering the depth of his despondency when he called and the hope he expressed at the end of our talk, I believe I had the privilege of being used as God's voice that night. After all, He has no hands or feet or voice on earth but ours. At the end of our conversation my friend was encouraged. The essence of the words spoken to him was later translated into this poetic expression, ***"Be Encouraged"***.

However, as I am preparing to include this piece in the book, I am saddened by the loss of a friend who committed suicide (November 2011). ***"Be Encouraged"*** is now dedicated to anyone who is on the brink of letting go or giving up on life.

Right now your situation and circumstance may seem desperately dark and immensely hopeless. You feel that life has dealt you a 'raw deal' and it isn't worth living through another day. But, for as low as you feel there is someone or something that can pull you back from this low place such as a loved one or a child. Think, now, of that person.

If you are contemplating taking your life, call a friend, a relative, a Pastor or dial 9-1-1 or your local emergency number RIGHT NOW!

BE ENCOURAGED

14 September 1993

You may be weighed down by past misfortunes
Tempted to believe life is but a game of luck and chances
Do not be restrained by failings or distresses from the past
Give God your today and tomorrows, in Him your plans will last

> Be encouraged through your struggles
> Let go of what you cannot change
> New possibilities are abounding
> Reset your target-range

When you cannot see beyond the pain, and tears your path obscure
Focus on the Almighty's promises; know that His words are sure
Know that your steps are ordered, lined-up with God's grand design
Though weapons formed they will not prosper, they will be realigned

> Be encouraged through your losses
> Wave sorrow and hurt good-bye
> Take pleasure in life's journey
> Through valleys-deep and mountains-high

When the enemy comes against you, overwhelming as a flood
Know that a standard has been raised; you're covered by the blood
Lean not on your own understanding; trust God with all your heart
Welcome each day's dawning; it's your chance for a new start

> Be encouraged through each downfall
> The good will outweigh the bad
> Count the blessings, not the shortfalls
> Then there'll be no room for sad

Nevertheless, Afterward

My Heart-Poem to God

Dearest Father,

It's me again. Today I stand in the gap for someone who cannot pray, someone who is desperate, someone on the verge of letting go. Abba, I do not know when this prayer will be needed or who will need it but I beseech You—in the name of Jesus—that this prayer, like a sped arrow, finds its target.

Daddy, You know, I've had dark days when living was too difficult and I was only kept from the alternative because it was too scary to do. In those days when I couldn't see beyond the dark clouds, You were there. When I couldn't pray, You understood my groaning and You were everything I needed even when I didn't know what I needed. You were the voice on a phone-call saying, "you were on my mind and I called to see how you are". You were the arm extended to hug me, and the hands extended to feed me. Yours were the feet that came bearing good tidings stopping the enemy from having his way.

Daddy, as You were to me, be the same and more to the person reading this who is about to give up.

You took me through the valley of the shadow of death and set me upon THE Rock, and I thank You from an exceedingly grateful heart. And if You did it for me, You can do it for anyone else. Do it now Father.

Always grateful,
Forever Yours,
Dee

Your Heart-Poem to God

Dear Reader

Regardless of how you are feeling—happy, sad, angry, disappointed etc.—it is important to acknowledge and give value to those feelings. God is interested in all your experiences. In the space below share with Him your feelings and make your requests known to Him.

Before Word

"And he said unto her, Daughter, thy faith hath made thee whole; go in peace, and be whole of thy plague." (Saint Mark 5:34, King James Version)

"And He took the damsel by the hand, and said unto her, talitha cumi; which is, being interpreted, Damsel, I say unto thee arise. And straightway the damsel arose and walked . . . ." (Saint Mark 5: 41-42, King James Version)

*T*he upcoming piece was written after an encounter with God during one of His 'silent moments' to my prayers and supplications. When He did respond, He directed me to the story of the woman with the "issue of blood" and in it I found encouragement.

You may be quite familiar with this story—this woman was bleeding for 12 years and by the time Jesus showed up in her story she had spent all of her resources on physicians and none helped her. In fact, when she showed up in Jesus' story, He was on His way to see about a 12 year old girl who was very sick to the point of death. The girl was Jairus' only child.

Being an only-child Himself, and also face-to-face with His own impending death, I believe this made Jesus even more resolute in His commitment to help the child. But, as He steadfastly made His way through the throng He felt virtue depart from His body that not only propelled Him to a standstill, but also caused an immediate cessation to the incessant bleeding.

And, in that moment while He sought to identify and then commend the one who touched Him with such faith, the child dies.

For 12 years this woman was losing her life-source. Her faith-action caused Jesus to stop long enough to affirm her faith and assure her healing, and in so doing the life of a 12-year-old girl ebbed away.

The twelve-years-life/twelve-years-death anomaly played over and over in my mind until I caught a glimpse of what God's heart was communicating to mine.

God's delay is not His denial or is His indifference to the issues we face; nor is His silence neglect. He is biding His time, patiently waiting for just the right moment to intercede. His time is not always our time and while He tarries, the promise may die and the enemy will rejoice. But that moment of 'dead promise' gives God a picture-perfect platform upon which to interject most efficaciously.

When Jesus eventually showed up in the little girl's story, He restores her life with two words—*"thalitha cumi"*.

Is He silent to you?
Are you crying out but you do not hear Him?
Be encouraged!
While He tarries, you wait.

At the fixed moment He will also call out to you: ***"Talitha Cumi"*** which means *"damsel arise"*, and straightway you too will rise to the reality that your promise, though it tarries, is not dead.

TALITHA CUMI

28 May 2006

I cry aloud O Lord, why do You not hear me?
My soul is empty, I yearn for You
Darkness blocks my path to You
I am lost without You

O Lord, Your coming in and going out, why are they hidden from me?
Behold, I go forward, I cannot find You
I go backward, I do not perceive You
Why do You hide Yourself, O Lord, from me?
If only I knew where I might find You
That I may plead my cause before You
With all that I am, beseech You

While the night shadows loom about me, O Lord
Will You not bring light to my path?

      Damsel, daughter, woman of God—arise!
      Your times are not hidden from Me
      This too shall pass, you will overcome
      I am your God
      I am Sovereign
      I am in control
      I embodied the boundlessness of My strength in you
      Deliberately calculated against My plan
      Measured to the span and frequency of My time

      Arranged all things—life's good and its bad—together for
          your good purpose
      So what if weeping comes?
      Morning's joy will follow

      Your night has ended
      Morning has come!

Good morning woman of God—arise!
The breaking of day is on its way
Reach out! Stretch your hands toward the heavens
Speak out! Release the hurt, the losses, the pain
Unleash heaven's blessings
Reclaim your virtuous place
Your worth is far above diamonds
I've likened you to My church
I gave the best of Me to redeem you
The enemy is defeated
An empty grave proves this is true

Arise woman of God—arise!
I conceived you in My mind
Designed you with My hands
Outlined intricately
Sketched precisely
Etched indelibly in My heart

Fashioned for a divine purpose
Conformed to My image
Lined up every circumstance
Orchestrated your experiences
Kept alive for such a time
For such a time as this

"Talitha cumi"
Damsel, daughter of God
It's morning
Arise!

Nevertheless, Afterward

My Heart-Poem to God

Dear Abba,

You gave me a sure word of promise that has been sustaining me. When the promise appears to be dying, remind me that it is You who said, ". . . though it tarries wait for it for it will surely come it will not tarry". Only You can bring agreement from incongruity. So I'll wait, even in the tarrying, for what You promise You also have the power to do; and this sure word of promise You gave me will surely come.

While I wait Father, encourage me. While the promise tarries and even dies, remind me that You are the restorer of dead things. And when You manifest this word in my life I will be mindful to give You all the honor and all the glory and all will know that You are indeed God!

I love You always
Dee

Your Heart-Poem to God

Dear Reader

May be you too are faced with a dead or dying promise. In the space below share with God the sentiments of your heart and beseech Him to extend virtue on your behalf.

Before Word

> *"Be still, and know that I am God; I will be exalted among the nations, I will be exalted in the earth."* (Psalm 46:10. King James Version)

> *"Be still before the Lord and wait patiently for him . . . ."* (Psalm 37:7, English Standard Version)

"Be Still" was written for a friend who was diagnosed with a life-threatening sickness in 2003 and who opted to trust God for her healing. What do you say to someone in the face of such faith? At the time two words came to mind—'be still'. The piece has been modified since, but the sentiment remains the same, to be still, and is also now dedicated to you.

To be still is to be in a place of inner quietude, or as David referred to it a time to *"commune with your own heart".* (Psalms 4:4, King James Version) However, to be still is more than a meditative state of being. It is a state of decisive intention to connect to the Power than is greater than you. To be still is to make a conscious decision to remove all external forces in full surrender to the Omnipresence of God in order to be 'at-one-ment' with Him, or to know Him. External forces such as fear, doubt, anger, worry and even family, friends and jobs will impede your ability to be still.

Maybe you are experiencing moments of chaos in your health, your finances, your relationships or on your job. In the noise of it all you cannot hear the voice of God. In this moment He invites you to be still and be encouraged as you wait on and for Him.

Dawn A. Minott

BE STILL

17 September 2003

Be still?

Lord, how can I be still while life rushes by?
Surely, "be still" was for a different time

When men and women heard Your voice
And a donkey talked for it had no choice

When a river's direction turned about
And a wall came down at the sound of a shout

When a sea parted for a mighty exodus
And healing took place from a faithful touch

When some who died were given life anew
And a man walked with You way beyond the blue

Certainly then Lord, but not now
Be still? Okay, but Lord, how?

    Be still—take time out, pause, be at rest in Me
        And when doubt and fear consume me?
    Be still—don't speak, be quiet, just listen for Me
        But Lord, I've tried yet I don't hear Thee
    Be still—do nothing, wait . . . wait for Me
        "I only have time, You have eternity"
    Be still—just trust Me

    When you say I am your Healer
    You are saying, *"you are healed"*!
    Be still then, sit at my feet and be renewed

When you say, I am your Provider
You are saying, *"you shall not want"!*
Be still then, abide in Me and be fulfilled

When you say I am your Shepherd
You are saying, *"you'll never be lost"!*
Be still then, wait awhile, know that I am God

Be still

Nevertheless, Afterward

My Heart-Poem to God

Hello Daddy,

How many times have I beseeched You for the gift of patience? It's been many, many, many times, eh?

Daddy, You know being still has been the biggest challenge for me 'cause I'm always thinking, doing, fixing, plotting. Even when I pray to You, I find myself trying to work "it" out.

Father, help me to be still—to be quiet long enough that I may hear You. Please give me also a willing heart that I may follow as You lead, not seeking my own way but wanting always to be in Your will.

And Daddy, no matter how much I whine and plead, grant me only those things by which You will be best served.

Thank You!

Forever Yours
Dee

Your Heart-Poem to God

Dear Reader

In the space below indicate the areas of your life you need to surrender to God and ask Him to help you to be patient—to be still—while He works it out. And, thank Him in advance for the victory.

Before Word

It is customary for us to ask *"how are you?"* when we meet an acquaintance, a friend, a co-worker or a fellow church member on the road, in the classroom, at church or in the hallway. Oft times it is flippant—we do not really wish to know how the person is doing, it is merely a form of greeting. So, before the response escapes their lips we are out of earshot and we hear what we expect to hear, *"I'm good"* or *"I'm OK"*, and we respond in the usual way, with a quick turn of the head: *"That's good"*.

On Tuesday, October 25th 2011 I greeted a co-worker with *"How are you?"* and the response was not the typical *"I'm good"* or *"I'm OK"*. Instead, it was: *"I'm depressed"*.

For someone to give such an honest response, it was evident that the pain was too immense to mask. And in that moment, Abba opened the opportunity to fulfill the request I make of Him in each morning's prayer: *"Please make me a blessing to someone today"*.

As it turned out, the young son of my co-worker's friend died suddenly—he was not sick, was not in an accident, he just died—and she was experiencing the loss as if it was her own and I felt and saw the immensity of her pain.

What do you say to comfort a mother when not only is she grieving for her friend's loss, but grieving with the reality that this too could happen to her own child? We prayed together and by the time I returned to my office, I was given these words of encouragement which I penned for her—**"When Answers Aren't Enough . . . JESUS is"**.

"Tomorrow There's No More Sorrow" was also written to encourage another friend who lost a loved one and was querying where God was during her time of loss.

WHEN ANSWERS AREN'T ENOUGH . . . JESUS IS

25 October 2011

Father

If it were not for Your mercy, where would we be
When the hearts of the young are failing
And they die before they've really lived

What do you say to a parent who's outlived their child?
A brother or sister who's lost a confidante, a friend?

What do you say to those separated by the finality of death?
To the one who empathizes through her own vulnerability?

In the moment when answers aren't enough Jesus is
His promises are sure

He promises to take the sting of death
He promises to give heavenly peace
He promises forever reunions
He promises eternal life
Weep for you must
Endure the night
In the morning
Will come
Joy

Dawn A. Minott

TOMORROW THERE'S NO MORE SORROW

11 December 1998

God is with you in your time of loss
He sees your pain and hears your cry

He feels the way your heart is breaking
He's wiping away your every tear

He hears your question, "Why me Lord?"
And whispers in His still-small voice

> It's not in my plan to see you hurt
> Nor suffer pain or sorrow
> Each time you cry
> It makes me sad
> For I, too, once suffered loss
> When upon that cross my only Child
> Though innocent He was
> Condemned to death for all the world
> He shed His precious blood
> It broke my heart when He agreed
> Not His will but mine be done
> For it meant I turned away, forsook Him
> 'Til His sacrifice was complete
>
> So, you see My child, I understand
> In this your time of loss
> My words are true, I promise you
> Tomorrow there'll be no more sorrow

Nevertheless, Afterward

My Heart-Poem to God

Abba,

Every passing of a loved-one is such a stark reminder that death is indeed the enemy for we were not created to die. But death is also a reminder of the ultimate death of Your Son, Jesus.

Father, I thank You for the plan of salvation through which You dissociated Yourself from Yourself so that You through Jesus could bear the eternal death for me; to be stricken and afflicted in order to bear my grief and carry my sorrow; to be wounded for my transgressions and bruised for my iniquities in order that I may be healed by Jesus' stripes. Thank You Jesus!

God, I stand in awe of You as Father, as Son and as Holy Spirit. I praise You and magnify You as Father, as Son and as Holy Spirit. There will never be enough tongues or enough words to fully express my gratitude for Your love and sacrifice.

Help me Father to live in each moment, knowing that death is the one sure thing in life. When death comes, I pray that it finds me contented in You.

Loving You in life to love You in eternity,

Forever Yours,
Dee

Your Heart-Poem to God

Dear Reader

In the space below share with God your experiences of loss and ask for His peace to be extended to your heart.

Before Word

*C*he United Nations benefit from a high-measure of security because of the humanitarian nature of its work. All this changed on August 19th in 2003 when a truck bomb was driven into the United Nations Headquarters in Bagdad and twenty-one persons were killed.

This reverberated throughout the halls of United Nations Offices all over the world—and in my case in Barbados where I was posted at the time—as staff expressed their shock, horror and sadness at what had happened.

The staff of the United Nations Headquarters in Barbados gathered two days later in a memorial service to honor those who made the ultimate sacrifice in the course of duty. *"In Memoriam"* was written for the occasion and read during the church service to encourage my fellow staff members.

Since 2003, the UN has increasingly become a target for attack, the latest being in Nigeria on August 26th, 2011 where twenty-three persons lost their lives.

I have since had occasion to visit the UN House in Nigeria and though the building remained unoccupied, at the entrance the reassembled plaque laid on a table. As I stood over it, it was a glaring reminder of the trauma of that day; but more importantly, the effort to reassemble it resonated as testimony to the resiliency of the staff—shattered but not broken.

"In Memoriam" is a tribute for colleagues who lost their lives in the line of duty; may their souls rest in peace.

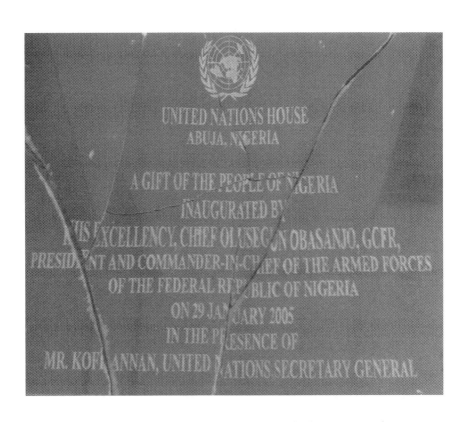

Photograph taken at UN House, Nigeria, by Dawn Minott

IN MEMORIAM

21 August 2003

Terror, like sharp arrows of the weak
Shattered the lives of our colleagues
The soul quivers within, distressed on every side
Those who survived wondering why
As they walk through the valley of the shadow of death
Lord, reveal Yourself as Warrior, Strong Tower and Defense

For them we raise our voice in prayer
We acknowledge You as Creator, Redeemer, Forgiver
Your ways are true, You are love, You reign in peace

To those who feel downtrodden and forsaken
Be the lifter of their hands
When doubt and fear compass their way
Be the restorer of their faith
Those who are sad, of a broken spirit
Shelter them in the pavilion of Your love
For You are protector, You are shield
Only in You will they find a safe retreat

Let the shrinking heart be strengthened
And the feeble mind made strong
For You O Lord, You are our comfort and our song

To you whose lives were snatched away
We pause in memory of your courage
You gave your all for a cause we must complete
Onward we'll continue to a future of peace

There are many enemies yet unknown
Let us learn to forgive, hold no hatred within
Let our hope rest only in You, Lord
Let our cry come near before You
And our hearts be strengthened by You
Protect us in our going out and in our coming in
O Lord, this is our humble prayer to thee

Nevertheless, Afterward

My Heart-Poem to God

Dear Abba,

Right after I finished University I expressed a desire of my heart. Daddy, You'll recall—I didn't kneel, clasped my hands or closed my eyes; I simply verbalized a desire of my heart: to work for the United Nations. And from my mouth to Your ears because a few months later I was in deed working for the UN.

Father, I thank You for allowing me to work for an organization with a global reach to address issues such as poverty, development, peace, security, human rights and justice for all.

I pray for Your protection over its staff who are often in harm's way to save and protect the lives of others. I pray for Your protection over this institution. I pray for Your direction to its leaders.

And Father I thank You for granting me my heart's desire which keeps me grounded in my career through the ups and downs, knowing that I am placed here for a purpose and will remain here until Your purpose is fulfilled in me.

Please help me to serve with honesty and integrity wherever You plant me.

Forever Yours,
Dee

Your Heart-Poem to God

Dear Reader

The space below is a good place to express your gratitude for the job you are blessed with or to request God's guidance in finding the right job for you if you are currently unemployed or looking for a change.

Before Word

*H*ave you heard someone say they were so low they'd have to look up to see bottom? Well, that is precisely how I felt on September 23rd in 2003. I remember that day vividly.

I was at a crossroads and completely bewildered about the direction my life should take. At the time I did not have a strong prayer life. Though I knew the mechanics of praying, I was clueless as to how to listen for the voice of God. But, I had run out of moves to direct my own life and knew enough about God to know that I could seek His guidance though I didn't know how to discern His answer.

So, I wrote down the six major areas of my life I needed Him to take full control of, and told Him I would stay in His Waiting Room until He told me to act; but that He'd have to be very clear in His response so I may know that He was indeed leading.

I don't recall the exact wording of my prayer but I knew I felt like a child who did not yet know how to walk; I needed step-by-step instruction. If memory serves me right, my prayer went something like this:

> *"Dear God, I know you are the God of Abraham and Isaac but today I need to know that You are **MY** God. I'm placing these six life-areas before you and I will not stop praying today until You answer me. In the same way you spoke to Moses and Abraham, I need You to speak to me **TODAY**".*

I would love to say I heard the audible voice of God that day, but I did not.

At the end of my prayer—actually it was more like my beseeching—I was impressed to open the Bible. I had never had a premonition like this before. It was such a strong intuition, and knowing what I had just requested in prayer, I was persuaded to believe it was a prompting from God. So, I opened the Bible. I had no idea what it would open to; and, when it did open I almost closed it in complete and utter disappointment because I was unequivocally-absolutely sure there was no way I would get the answer I needed from God in the book of Habakkuk!

"Habakkuk?!" I queried out loud in defiance.

Prior to that day, if I were asked to go to the book of Habakkuk I would first have to search for the page number in the table of contents. Yet, there I was, prostrate on my knees, with Habakkuk chapters 1, 2 and 3 opened before me. And again that strong impression came, commanding me to read.

"Read where?"

"Start from the beginning", came the impression.

So I started to read: Habakkuk chapter 1, verse 1; and no sooner than I got to verse 5 than I started arguing with God:

> *"I've come to You for answers to guide my life and You sent me to Habakkuk! And now I'm reading this Book and it's all about chastisement and judgment."*

Once more I was about to close the Bible and yet again the impression came, stronger, compelling me to read on. So, reluctantly I did. Then I got to Chapter 2, verse 1 and the words resonated with my spirit. That was exactly how I felt—I was challenging God to see what He was about to do with my request. Then when I read verses 3 and 4, it's as if God said: *"this is My word to you!"*

> *"For the vision is yet for an appointed time, but at the end it shall speak, and not lie: though it tarry, wait for it; because it will surely come, it will not tarry . . . . But the just shall live by his faith."* (Habakkuk 2:3-4, King James Version)

I experienced an assurance I had never felt before—my anxieties relaxed into peace; all the uncertainty about the future melted away.

I knew then that God heard me and this was His answer. So, I claimed it as my "sure" word and asked if He'd use Habakkuk 2:3 as confirmation whenever He was answering any of these six areas of my life. I have since replaced "vision" with "promise". This has been my sure-word of promise.

I kept on reading. Habakkuk closes with this declaration:

> *"The Lord God is my strength, and He will make my feet like hinds' feet, and He will make me to walk upon mine high places."* (Habakkuk 3:19, King James Version)

I was intrigued. *"Why 'hinds' feet, Lord?"*

The hind is a female red deer. I've since discovered that this kind of deer lives in the high mountains and easily and quickly moves across the uneven terrains and rock surfaces. She leaps from rock to rock without losing footing. Why? Because she places her rear feet in the exact same place where her front feet have just been to ensure she is surefooted as she navigates her home—the high places of the mountainous landscape.

Space will not allow me to share with you how God has been positioning me in my "high places" in providing answers to five of the six life-areas I placed before Him. On life-area six I continue to stay in God's Waiting Room. September 23rd, 2012 marked 9 years of waiting; He's given assurances along the way but the "promise" tarries. My faith has waned, and in those times I took matters in my hand and have failed and been hurt.

Now, I'm back in God's Waiting Room, waiting in hope against hope with a renewed faith that though the promise tarries, it will surely come. I will live on the basis of what God said He would do. From that new determination, *"Hope, Wait, Trust"* was written.

HOPE, WAIT, TRUST

28 August 2012

What is that thing most desired
That God seems not to grant?
Time passes, hope fritters away
Wait for hope in waiting
His promise is "yes" and in Him so will it be
'Twill be fulfilled in its appointed time
Though it tarries, **HOPE**, it will surely come

     He who promises cannot lie
     In quiet patience wait upon His word
     Keep steadfast watch, never faltering
     He returns by way of promises made
     With confidence unswerving
     He will do just what He said
     Though it tarries, **WAIT**, it will surely come

          Blessed you are for you believed
          Held steadfast to His word, not doubting
          Believing against all odds, not fearing
          Knowing He who promised is faithful
          A performance for all to see
          His promise you will receive
          Though it tarries, **TRUST**, it will surely come

Nevertheless, Afterward

My Heart-Poem to God

Daddy,

I know Your time is not my time and what You will do You will do on Your timetable. Honestly, sometimes I feel a need to remind You that You exist in infinity while I'm limited by the finiteness of time. A part of me cries out "when?"

Daddy, while the promise tarries, I will hope again, I will wait and I will trust You to do as You have said.

Forever Yours,
Dee

Your Heart-Poem to God

Dear Reader

Maybe you too have run ahead of God in certain areas of your life and now you wish to give up having your way and being subject to Him. If so, use the space below to let Him know that you too will trust Him and will wait for His plan to be manifested in your life.

CHAPTER 4

GOD MOMENTS

$\mathcal{T}$here are moments that are descried as "happenstances" and others as "coincidences", but those who are on the path to knowing the heart of God recognize these as "God moments".

God moments mark the times when the ordinary of our lives is interrupted and interjected with the extraordinary. They are moments that cannot be explained, or are so perfectly orchestrated they are truly too good to be of man and must therefore be of God.

God moments come whenever:

-   Like a (.) period: forcing us to stop and acknowledge that the normalcy and routine of our lives have been interrupted by the supernatural.
-   Like a (,) comma: causing us to pause in contemplative wonderment at what has just transpired.
-   Like an (!) exclamation: a ha-ha moment when we're awed into speechlessness or wonderment.
-   Like a (?) question mark: compelling us to query the depth and height of God's love measured in the magnitude of our capacity to stray in the face of His resolute determination to chase.
-   Like a (–) dash: betwixt and between the last dollar and an empty cupboard, a phone call to say "hey" breaking through a lonely moment, or the simultaneous pairing of the perfect song with the bewilderment of your heart.

God moments happen wherever, while we are taking a walk, driving on the busy thoroughfares or flying in the boundless skies.

And, no matter when or where they are manifested, we are caught off guard by God moments. But no, not so for God, these moments are all part of His design. And, He smiles a smile so big it lights up the sky as He savors our astonishment to His interspersing humanity with snippets of the Divine.

Enter now on the path to **God Moments!**

Before Word

*I*f you know me any at all, you will not be surprised by this declaration: I love the Psalmist David! In fact, I often say to my friends: *when we get to heaven if you're ever looking for me and I'm not sitting enthralled at the feet of Jesus, I'll be with David lost amidst the tall grasses in a beautiful meadow by the Sea of Glass—he'll be strumming the harp and I'll be composing a psalm.*

As I'm on this journey to know the heart of God, I grew to love David first because he was the most-real person in the Bible to me—I could relate to him. Others messed up, but David's life was the epitome of mess. But, through the lessons learned from his MESS, David composed MESSages—one hundred and fifty of them! I also love him because he was a connoisseur of words. In the composition of these messages, I admire the ways in which he creatively manipulated words to denote both their aesthetic and evocative meaning.

Most importantly, my love for David stems from the reality that in spite of the mess he got into, God could still testify that David was a man after his own heart (Acts 13:22). And notice, God didn't just say (speak, utter, articulate or express) it, God **testified** (gave evidence, bore witness, swore, affirmed) it. Amazingly, God testified this not before David messed up, but after!

For me, during my tumultuous-see-saw-like ways of journeying to the heart of God, I was very much encouraged by David. Through David's experiences I was reminded that God is always chasing after me. If He's chasing, it means I'm running away from Him. In other words, I didn't just come to God; I was drawn to Him by His everlasting love and loving kindness (Jeremiah 31:3). Yes, I submitted but He first "drew me" into relationship with Him so I may, in time, look like Him. And, so it is with you—you run, God chases; you submit, God abides; you're changed.

Just like He testified of David, I now live in the anticipation of hearing God testify of me saying: *"Dawn's heart looks like My heart"*.

So, it was in one of these moments when my mind transported me to our time in heaven where David and I are lost in the creative process of composing a psalm commemorating the depth and height of God's love measured in the magnitude of our capacity to stray in the face of His resolute determination to chase, that ***"The One Hundred and Fifty-first Psalm"*** was composed.

Wouldn't it be amazing if I would remember this composition in the earth-made-new and recite it to David? I wonder what he would think of his little sister's attempt to model him in being a Psalmist.

THE 151ST PSALM

30 August 2002

Section I

¹ Oh Lord, my Lord
How manifold is Your creative power
Manifested in everything around me

² In all that I can touch, and see, and feel
Lord, You are there

³ Even when I'm alone with the night
My God, the stars, the moon, they testify of You

⁴ Distinctive voices You gave the creatures of the night
A croaking, hissing, whistling serenade

⁵ Dawn uncloaks night-time darkness
Awaking the day
Dew drops glistening from sun's first ray

⁶ Babbling brooks, flowing oceans
Great mountains, deep valleys
Welcomes my soul's retreat to nature's peaceful escape

⁷ Oh Lord, my Lord
How manifold is your creative power
I am intrigued by You

Section II

[8] To You alone I will raise my voice and sing
      Praise and adoration, I magnify You
      You alone are King

[9] Creator, Redeemer, Almighty
      You, oh Lord, are Sovereign
      Worthy are You

[10] You reign in peace
      Your ways are true
      You are love

[11] I extend my praise to reach Your throne above
      I dance with exceedingly great joy before you

[12] When I am downtrodden and forsaken
      You are the lifter of my hand
      When doubt and fear compass my way
      You are the restorer of my faith
      When I am sad and of a broken spirit
      You envelope me in the pavilion of Your love

[13] You are my Protector
      You are my Shield
      Only in You will I find a safe retreat

[14] Oh Lord, my Lord
      How manifold is Your saving power
      I am redeemed by You

Section III

¹⁵ Though sorrow comes to cloud my way
    I look to You, the Light

¹⁶   Sickness comes, for sin must have its way
    I am restored by Your stripes
    You, oh Lord, are Life
    It is in You that I live

¹⁷ How can I not extol You above the heavens and praise You upon
    the earth?
    In times of joy, in times of sadness, in times of peace, in
        times of war
    When my enemies descend upon me, even then will I praise
        You
    For You hold my times in your hands

¹⁸ Lord, let me not withhold my praise from You
    But with joy and thanksgiving be constant in adoration and
        worship
    Let me sing of Your goodness and testify of Your love
    For You alone, oh Lord, is worthy and deserving of my praise

¹⁹ Come, all ye earth, let our music glorify Him
    Let our hosannas loudly ring, soaring in praise to our King
    The earth will tremble and the wicked will be moved
    As in triumph we sing hallelujahs to Him

²⁰ He who gained victory o'er the grave
    Listen, for lo, all creation testifies that He alone is Lord
    Worthy of praise, worthy of glory, worthy of honor
    Let the shrinking heart be strengthened
    And the feeble mind be made strong

²¹ Oh lord, my Lord
    How manifold is your restoring power
    I am captivated by You

Before Word

*T*he more I think on why I pray, the more I come to realize that my prayers are really but fragments of my heart when I'm compelled to stop in acknowledgement that the normalcy and routine of my life has been interrupted by the supernatural. Like when my eyes open in the morning and I realize that I'm alive, the fragment of gratitude from my heart escapes upon my lips: *"thank you Father for waking me up".*

WITH ALL THERE IS TO SAY TO GOD—

the thanksgiving, the praising, the adoration, the questioning;
the joy, the sorrow, the loss, the longing, the hurting;
the wonderings and what-ifs, the near-misses and
could-have-been;

my prayers are unending conversations taking place with:
eyes-wide-open, eyes-tightly-closed;
standing-up, kneeling-down;
hands clasped or held high;

filled with emotions seen in:
tears of joy or tears of sadness;
unending smiles and abandoned laughter;
sometimes loud and sometimes soft;
sometimes no words at all just groans;

transpiring while:
folding laundry;
washing dishes;
walking;
or jogging;

—MY HEART REVEALS UNENDING **"FRAGMENTS OF PRAYER"**.

FRAGMENTS OF PRAYER

8 April 2009

It's while I'm standing still in traffic Lord
And all others are restless around me
I'll take the time to speak to You
A fragment of my heart

It's in the office when things go awry Lord
No matter what strategies we try
I'll take the time to share with You
A fragment of my heart

It's when I sit in church Lord
And close my eyes for just a while
I'll take the time to speak to You
A fragment of my heart

Whether it be surreal like a dream Lord
Or the day is filled with the bustle of life
I'll take the time to share with You
A fragment of my heart

If the answers come straight away or be delayed Lord
And anxiety sets in while I wait
I'll take the time to speak to You
A fragment of my heart

Make each fragment of my petition whole Lord
Then as I lay upon my bed I'll rest in content
Knowing You've made complete my heart's desires
From fragments of prayers

Before Word

"My sheep listen to My voice; I know them, and they follow Me." (Saint John 10:27, New International Version)

"We all, like sheep, have gone astray, each of us has turned to our own way . . . ." (Isaiah 53:6, New International Version)

"They reel to and fro, and stagger like a drunken man, and are at their wit's end." (Psalm 107:27, King James Version)

𝒯he 23rd Psalm is probably one of the best-known Psalms written by David. The sentiments of the Psalm leave no doubt that he wrote it from the experience of a "God moment"—a moment which caused him to pause in contemplative wonderment at what had just transpired. Maybe it was written after he killed the bear or the lion with his bare hands in defense of the sheep he was tending. (1 Samuel 17:34-35)

In reading this Psalm I experienced a ha-ha moment when I came face-to-face with the realization that whatever I say God is; then, I must see myself in relation to that attribute. For instance, if I say He is my "Shepherd"; then, I must be assured that I am His "sheep" and live in that assurance.

I was curious as to why David wrote this Psalm. The obvious reason is that David tended sheep so it makes good sense for him to use the analogy of sheep and shepherd. However, in researching the characteristics of a sheep, I saw clearly why God likened humanity to sheep (Isaiah 53:6), and why this inspired David's 23rd Psalm.

In all that I learned about sheep, the most intriguing finding was this—a sheep is easily "cast". That is the term used by shepherds for a sheep that has turned over on its back. A casted sheep cannot right itself and could starve to death or become easy prey if not righted again. A casted sheep is fully dependent on the shepherd to rescue it.

Have you ever been "cast" down, in a rut or at a loss at wit's-end crossroads and there is nothing you can do to right yourself? I have. And, it was in one of these moments when, like David, I beseeched: *"why are you downcast, O my soul? Why so disturbed within me?"* (Psalm 45:5, New International Version) that God invited me to act on my faith in believing He is my Shepherd and as such to live in the assurance that I am His "sheep".

It is in seeing me as a "cast sheep", in claiming God as my "Shepherd", and in resting in the assurance that He has the ability to right me that *"A Sheep's Look at the Shepherd's Psalm"* was conceptualized.

Dawn A. Minott

A SHEEP'S LOOK AT THE SHEPHERD'S PSALM

1 October 2011

The Lord is my Shepherd . . . that's parenting
I shall not want . . . that's adequacy
He makes me . . . that's submission
To lie down . . . that's rest
In green pastures . . . that's comfort

He leads me . . . that's direction
Beside the still waters . . . that's relaxation
He restores my soul . . . that's rejuvenation
He leads me . . . that's guidance
In paths of righteousness . . . that's grace
For His name's sake . . . that's adoption

Yeah, though I walk . . . that's assertion
Through the valley . . . that's protection
Of the shadow of death . . . that's releasing **F**alse **E**vidence
which **A**ppears **R**eal
I will fear no evil . . . that's trust
For He is with me . . . that's assurance
His rod and staff . . . that's correction
Comfort me . . . that's solace

He prepares a table before me . . . that's provision
In the presence of mine enemies . . . that's embolden audacity
He anoints my head with oil . . . that's consecration
My cup runs over . . . that's abundance

Surely . . . that's superlative guarantee
Goodness and mercy shall follow me . . . that's justification
All the days of my life . . . that's sanctification
I will dwell in the house of the Lord forever . . . that's
glorification

Selah . . . pause now, contemplate

Before Word

$\mathcal{T}$he Bible is replete with the use of the number 7. It has been argued that the number 7 is associated with Divine completion and spiritual perfection, and aptly so. Examples to substantiate this argument include:

- The world was created in 7 days—**complete and perfect creation!** (Genesis 1 & 2)
- The week culminates on the 7th day, the Sabbath—**complete and perfect week & rest!** (Genesis 2:1-2)
- Samson's locks were braided in 7 plaits—**complete and perfect strength!** (Judges 16:13)
- Naaman, the leper, was cleansed only after he dipped in the Jordan River the 7th time—**complete and perfect healing!** (2 Kings 5:10)
- Jesus spoke 7 times from the cross—**complete and perfect salvation!** (Saint John 19:26, 28 & 30; Saint Luke 23:34, 43 & 46; Saint Matthew 27:46)
- The words "be still" appear together 7 times *(in King James Version)*—**complete and perfect quietude!** (1 Kings 22:3; Psalms 4:4; Psalms 46:10; Psalms 84:4; Isaiah 23:2; Jeremiah 47:6; Saint Mark 4:39)
- The greatest recorded miracle of Jesus, resurrecting Lazarus from death, is recorded as the 7th miracle in the book of Saint John—**complete and perfect miracle!** (Saint John 11:1-44)
- In the last book of the Bible, Revelation, there are 7 blessings, 7 churches, 7 candlesticks, 7 seals and 7 angels—**complete and perfect redemption!** (Revelation 1:3, 14:13, 16:15, 19:9, 20:6, 22:7, 22:14); (Revelation 1:11); (Revelation 1:12); (Revelation 6:1-17, 8:1-5); (Revelation 1:20, 8:6)

However, for me, the ha-ha moment was the intriguing discovery of the use of the number 7 in the Book of Saint John where Jesus describe Himself using "I AM" 7 times to help us understand the

complete and perfect incarnation wherein God became one of us, to be one with us, in order that He may save us.

He said:

1. *"I am the bread of life* . . . ." (Saint John 6:35, King James Version)
2. *"I am the light of the world* . . . ." (Saint John 8:12, English Standard Version)
3. *"I am the door* . . . ." (Saint John 10:9, King James Version)
4. *"I am the good shepherd* . . . ." (Saint John 10:11, New International Version)
5. *"I am the resurrection, and the life* . . . ." (Saint John 11:25, King James Version)
6. *"I am the way, and the truth, and the life* . . . ." (Saint John 14:6, English Standard Version)
7. *"I am the true vine* . . . ." (Saint John 15:1. English Standard Version)

The moment I came to the realization that I will never be able to fully understand or describe God, and thankfully so because if I could then He would cease to be God, the upcoming piece was born as a tribute to God for who and what He is—the *"I Am"*. There are parts of the piece that were inspired by the creative expressions of my friend and spiritual motivator, Andrew Adar.

I AM

4 July 2008

Yahweh, if there was another who had such love
    I would honor that god
Jehovah, if there was another who had such power
    I would worship that god
Adonai, if there was another who had such magnificence
    I would praise that god

But, in all the universe there is
    None as loving
    None as powerful
    None as magnificent as You
    You alone are the only true God

There is none who commands the heavens
There is none who creates and recreates
There is none who dies so He may save
There is none who bears the scars to the width and breadth of His
    love like You

You are the lavishly-adoring, love-engraving, scar-bearing, cross-
    carrying, emptying-Yourself-of-everything, forgive-them-while-
    You're-bleeding God

You are the ridiculously-creative, universe-out-of-nothing, galaxy-
    shaping, real-big-bang, the-original-"Discovery-Channel"-making
    God

You are the out-of-dirt-body-forming, kneel-in-the-dust-and-make-
    man-look-like-Him, kiss-of-life-breathing God

You are the time-space-continuum-defying, here-there-everywhere-ever-
    present, all-knowing-all-powerful-infinite-transcendent-immanent
    God

Though I can't ever get anything right
    Though I can do no good thing
        Though I am stubborn, stiff-necked, prone to stray
           Though I hurt You time and time again

Yet, You, the all-powerful God declares:
I am Your child, I am Your name, Your reputation, Your image
I am Your crown, I am Your glory, Your honor, Your love
I am the proof that You are who You say You are

You are:
Creator! Redeemer! Saviour! Sanctifier!
Keeper! Sustainer! Provider! Shelter!
Refiner! Life-giver! Vindicator! Negotiator!
Comforter! Strengthener! Restorer! Redeemer!
Beauty-for-ashes, joy-for-mourning, praise-for-brokenness Exchanger!

You are:
Brother yet Father! Judge yet Advocate!
First yet Last! Beginning yet End!
Lily yet Rose! Bread yet Water!
Giver yet Taker! Sword yet Shield!
Branch yet Root! High-Priest yet Sacrifice!
Shepherd yet Lamb! Man yet God!

How can this be?

Because
    You are God, besides You there is no other
    You exist by Yourself and for Yourself
    You are independent of any source, entity or concept
    You are uncreated and ongoing
    You are the quintessence God
    You are
    The
    I AM

Before Word

*C*he upcoming piece was conceptualized when I contemplated —what if Hell (the devil) and Death (the ultimate enemy) could have had a conversation when Jesus died and was buried, what might it have been like?

The result is the allegory, *"The Master Key"*, which is also my tribute to the cross.

The cross symbolizes the extent of God's love embodied in the death His Son, Jesus Christ, stretched out and extended from one pierced hand to the other for me. For, if I were the only one to have sinned, the plan of salvation would still have been unfolded in order that God could save only me.

Through Jesus' death and resurrection, hell and death are defeated so we may live in the confidence that He is *"The Master Key"!*

Only He can lock and unlock the circumstances of your life. What He closes, no one can open; and what He opens, no one can close because Jesus is *"The Master Key"*. And this fact is the epitome of a "God moment" which should cause us to pause in contemplative wonderment.

THE MASTER KEY

8 July 2004

Imagine . . .

It's early Sunday morning. "Hell" and "Death" are pacing back and forth, restlessly monitoring the tomb that previously belonged to Joseph of Arimathaea but now encloses the body of Jesus Christ.

Nervously, they had watched for signs throughout Friday night—nothing happened. Then the Sabbath drew on and . . . nothing. As the Sabbath wore on, their confidence grew, for still nothing happened. All throughout Saturday night they watched and listened . . . nothing happened.

But, early Sunday morning, just at the dawning of the day, a sound was heard. It was only audible to someone on the watch—"someone" like Hell and "someone" like Death.

Hell: What is that I hear? Death, I thought you said you had Him?

Death: Well, of course I have Him, I even have the key!

Hell: Don't you mean "our key", the key of hell and death?

Death: Listen. It's faint right now, but with each beat it's steadily strengthening
I am absolutely sure, I can hear it now, His heartbeat is returning

Hell: He mustn't leave that tomb
If He does, our fate will be forever doomed

Death: I was there all Friday evening, I had to see
         He hung His head in full surrender to me
         I didn't leave His side 'til I was sure He was mine
         I saw His Father's confirmation in the earth and in
             the sky

Hell: Oh yes, it was a magnificent moment when I heard
             his pitiful cry:
         "Father . . . my Father . . . Your only Son You will
             deny?"
         Finally, after waiting and plotting this sweet
             life-wrenching revenge
         Lifeless, suspended between heaven and my hell, hung
             the One who was my challenge

Death: I thought He would have fought me, like so many
             others before
         But, it's as if He took His life and decidedly laid it at
             my door

         I wanted Him to struggle against my stranglehold on
             Him
         But, He acted more like a victor, accepting the
             ultimate penalty for humanity's sin

Hell: Be silent Death! No more time to reminisce
         This man . . . the Christ . . . He is our nemesis!
         No time to think of what could be or what we
             didn't do
         His life is returning, His heartbeat's reverberating
             from the tomb

Death: Hurry your "evilness", to the tomb of the Nazarene!
         He must not be raised or He will take away our key
         Together we rule this earth, this is our domain
         Who is this man to think we'd allow Him to live
             again?

As if on cue, Gabriel—heaven's Archangel—stands before Hell and Death garbed in the majesty of heaven. Staring them squarely in the eyes and with the adoration of the heavenly hosts embodied within him, exclaimed as like a song:

Gabriel: Who is this man?

He is the only Son of God, begotten from the world's foundation

He is the Rock of Ages upon which will be your eternal destruction

He is the Conquering Lion, Jesus Christ, humanity's redemption

He is the Good Shepherd, in Him there is no consternation

He is the First the Last, the Last the First, in Him there is continuation

He is the Beginning and the End, the Way and the Resurrection

He is Elohim. Shalom. Jireh. Rapha. Raah.

He is El-Shaddai. Adonai. Nissi. Rohi. Jah.

He is the God/Man—Jesus Christ the Savior!

And with a voice penetrating the hollow of the tomb, Gabriel shouts the Father's command:

Jesus!
Arise!
Stand up!
Come forth!
Your Father calls You home!

But Hell was not ready to concede. He positioned himself before the tomb and beckoned Death to join him.

Hell: This cannot be, only I have the key
               The key to hell and death and I will not concede to
                   thee
               Death, bind Him closer, hold Him, don't you dare let
                   Him leave
               He, and all humanity, must surrender and worship the
                   god in me

While Hell and Death held on to the last shreds of
their short-lived victory, Jesus adhered to His Father's
call; He unwrapped the shroud; stepped forth as the
Conquering Lion of the Tribe of Judah; and in a voice
clear, majestic and triumphant proclaimed:

Jesus: Oh Death, where is your sting, and Hell your victory?
               Did you really think My Father would allow you to
                   conquer Me?
               Now recognize I am He—He who has the master key
               Through my life, you're both condemned for all
                   eternity

               Did you not hear, when it was declared I am the Way
                   and Life?
               My life I laid down at the cross, to save the world
                   from sin's strife
               Did you not hear when Gabriel declared My Father
                   called me home?
               My life I take up, I'm heaven-bound to sit at the right
                   hand of His throne

And looking down through the portals of time to you and me,
Jesus exclaimed:

               Dear children of mine, don't despair even in the
                   darkest night
               At the break of dawn I'll return to take you home on
                   a cosmic flight

For I am He, He who was dead, now I'm alive
    forevermore
Hell and Death will be devoured in the lake of fire I
    have in store

So, Death where is your sting and Hell your victory?
I'm on the way to Heaven, I AM the MASTER KEY!

Before Word

Question: How does one identify someone who is a Christian or Christ-like?

Answer: By their "fruit"-actions.

> *"Yes, just as you can identify a tree by its fruit, so you can identify people by their actions."* (Saint Matthew 7:20, New Living Translation)

$\mathcal{A}$ Christian, then, is someone whose life is governed by the Spirit of God and will demonstrate the *"fruit of the Spirit [which] is love, joy, peace, longsuffering, gentleness, faith, meekness, temperance".* (Galatians 5:22-23, King James Version) Notice, the Bible verse used fruit in the singular form. However, it is a fruit with multiple parts. Like an orange, it is one fruit with many pegs.

Have you observed that the pegs of an orange are never all the same size? So it is with my "fruit"/character.

As a child of God, surrendered to His will, I am endowed with the character of the Spirit called "fruit" which has multiple "pegs"/ traits. So, I have a "peg" of love, and a "peg" of joy and peace and longsuffering and gentleness and faith and meekness and temperance. But, as I traverse this journey to knowing the heart of God, there have been many times when a "peg"/trait or two of my "fruit"/ character have been smaller than others in that I've been impatient, intemperate, less than loving and not always kind. I remain a "fruit". In other words, I remain a child of God, i.e. a Christian. What it means, however, is that there are some traits in me that need strengthening and that I cannot do on my own. I need the Divine Gardner to build me up and He is always ready to heed my call for "peg"-restoration.

He reminds me that being like Him is a daily process of complete dependence on Him, like a casted sheep, in order that I may exhibit all traits of the Spirit in the same measure. Of course, there will be times when I will fall. God acknowledges that. He states: *". . . a righteous man may fall seven times . . ."* However, knowing His power to sustain, God did not end it there, He goes on to say *". . . and rises again".* (Proverbs 24:16, New King James Version)

God is ever ready to pick us up and to strengthen the small/ under-developed "pegs"/traits of our "fruit"/character.

The forthcoming poem, *"The Fruit of the Spirit is . . . JOY & PEACE",* was written for and recited at a church convention in Barbados where the focus was on "joy and peace". It is a reminder that at the start of each day, in the tranquility of dawn, it is a good opportunity to start anew and to allow the Holy Spirit to fill us up so we exhibit each trait of love, joy, peace, longsuffering, gentleness, faith, meekness and temperance to those with whom we come in contact.

Dawn A. Minott

THE FRUIT OF THE SPIRIT IS . . . JOY & PEACE

30 November 2007

Early morn, day lays waiting
Darkness abounds where moonlight's hiding

Nighttime creatures' chatter pierce the calm
Tree branches whisper heaven's lullaby

Humanity surrendered in death-like slumber
No senseless babble, no unrest, no distress

Amidst the calm it can be heard
The Savior's gentle voice inviting

Sleep to forfeit, to sit at His feet
It's time for choosing

Before dawn ushers in the day
Too busy to love, gain joy or peace
To be gentle, longsuffering or kind
Must finish this task, meet with the boss
No meekness or goodness in mind

> While day is breaking
> It's time for choosing JOY and PEACE

> Before the enemy can have his way
> To JOY and PEACE commit the day

> In all doings, give God praise
> With JOY and PEACE heart and voice raise

In all choices, seek God's face
For JOY and PEACE to run life's race

When daily tasks are finally done
In JOY and PEACE lay you down

In the calm of it all, hear it inviting
The Savior's gentle voice calling

Sleep to forfeit, to sit at His feet
It's time again for choosing

Nevertheless, Afterward

My Heart-Poem to God

Abba,

You have revealed Yourself to me in myriads of ways, it truly does boggle my mind that You are so interested in me.

Thank You for the many moments when You punctuated my drab reality with the pure delight of Your God-ness.

Thank You for being my Shepherd. Like a sheep I have gone astray, I've had my own way, but You kept chasing after me. Thank You for bringing me into an understanding of the boundlessness of Your love in wanting to save me. You've been most patient and kind with Your messages of chastisement. You've been so gentle in Your chastening and very generous in Your loving.

Daddy, for every time I broke Your heart, I'm sorry, please forgive me. For every time I stray, come find me, please don't ever leave me.

O Love that will not let me go, I love You.

Forever Yours,
Dee

Your Heart-Poem to God

Dear Reader

I know you've experienced God moments even if you may not be aware of them, like just before or after something dramatic or traumatic happens and you exclaim: "Oh my God!"

Use the space below to share with God your gratitude for those OMG moments when He interceded in the normalcy of your life and interjected some "God moments".

CHAPTER 5

MIRACULOUS MOMENTS

$\mathcal{A}$ccording to the Oxford Dictionary, a miracle is *"an extraordinary and welcome event that is not explicable by natural or scientific laws and is therefore attributed to a divine agency"*.

On this last chapter of the journey, I wish to focus on the miracles that form the basis of my Christian faith. There would be no need for me to journey to the heart of God if there was not:

- the miracle of immaculate conception;
- the miracle birthed from barren and virgin wombs;
- the miracle of God becoming man;
- the miracle coalesced in grace, mercy and love;
- the miracle of grace and the gift of eternal life; and
- the ultimate miracle—the culmination of all miracles—the 2nd return of Jesus to the earth.

Enter now on the path to **Miraculous Moments!**

Before Word

The Miracle of Immaculate Conception

*C*hristianity is the only religion based on a God who made Himself less than Deity to become one with a people who had flagrantly rebelled against Him and, who would ultimately kill Him. Knowing this, yet He made Himself a fetus and placed Himself in the womb of a virgin woman who He Himself had created to be nurtured by the things He Himself had made so that he could be born as a man in order to save humankind. Does that baffle your mind? It completely boggles mine!

So mysterious is the miracle of Immaculate Conception—all of humanity's ability to comprehend brought together to contemplate it for as long as time exists would never be enough to explain this phenomenon. On the other side of this miracle is Mary, the woman chosen to be the mother of the Messiah.

Have you ever wondered what it was like for Mary being the mother of Jesus?

Imagine her astonishment first when an angel visits her, and then when he pronounced that she would be the mother of the Messiah. This is a prophecy she heard from her earliest days and knew that her people were long awaiting the Messiah who would be born of a virgin; and now she's been told, she is that virgin.

May be she wondered:

- *How do I raise a baby who is God and is therefore my creator yet I'm to be His mother?*
- *Would He cry at birth signaling His entry into the world He created?*
- *Would He suffer from childhood illnesses?*
- *Would He fit in with other children?*
- *Would He be shy or extraverted?*

-    *Would I teach Him about God, His Father, or would He teach me?*
-    *Would I be a good mother?*

And can you imagine the horror she experienced when she realized He was not among the throng returning home from the temple in Jerusalem that fateful day?

With each worried-emphatic callout: *"Jesus! Jesus! Where are you?"* her anxiety rose as adrenalin pulsated through her veins pressing her retreat back to the temple. With each hurried step, flashback to the time of Herod's determination to kill her child played o'er and o'er in her mind. Did she wonder with each step if she had failed the mission to protect the Son of God?

And as her child grew older, edging closer and closer to his 33rd year, did she wonder if she'd be able to let go knowing His death was imminent and then He'd return to His Father in heaven, leaving her on earth?

"Mary's Awesome Child" was conceived as I pondered Mary's life from the time of the angel's visit to the expectation of seeing her Son again on His second return to earth, not as her baby but as her King.

Dawn A. Minott

MARY'S AWESOME CHILD

23 February 1999

In the still of the night
A light so bright
From sleep awakens me
Unsure and afraid, I look around to see
God's holy angel standing by
With a solemn mission I could not deny

Me, you want me to be the mother of the Messiah?
It would be my heart's desire
To play a role in Redemption's plan
A plan to save the soul of everyone

And so the Holy Spirit gently came
My life has not been the same
For within my womb was placed God's only Son Almighty
Nine months to protect and keep in safety

But, how do I tell my husband-to-be
There is already a child inside of me?

I know—I'll say:

He will be called the Prince of Peace
His name to all a sweet release
God, becoming a child like no other
To Him we'll be father and mother
To nurture, protect and to teach the way
To hear His first word and to watch Him play

I'll cradle Him safe upon my breast
To Him I'll be a mother best
After Him my womb will bear none other
So awesome, like Christ, to call me mother

Donkeys, horses in a barn
All beheld God's miracle being born
Pharisees and Scribes too blind to see
That the prophecy of the Messiah had come to be

Wise men traveled from afar
And shepherds followed a distant star
Bowed down their heads to worship Him
But Herod tried to have Him killed
From Bethlehem's manger we had to flee
Our child, indeed, would be a Nazarene

And Jesus increased in wisdom and stature
Spending many days alone with God in nature
An understanding of scriptures beyond His years
He challenged the doctrine of even those who weren't His peers

I remember—I lost Him once among a worshiping throng
Three days I worried and searched—where did I go wrong?
When I found Him He was carrying out His Father's affair
Speaking with an authority, learnt men revere

Returning home, I held tightly to His hand
My heart is heavy, now I truly understand
Today, three days lost in a crowd
Tomorrow, three days in a grave enshroud

No longer a child, but a man of thirty years
With a hug and a kiss, He left me in tears
He traveled near and far from home
Without a place to call His own

I remember His first miracle—turning water into wine
So proud was I, for once upon a child He was mine
Stories came from every corner
So many miracles and yet they wondered
If He was the promised King, their Messiah
No! Too lowly and humble to be their Deliverer

And so, my child they nailed up, upon a tree
But before He died He looked out to me
For He could always see deep within my heart
And He knew just then it was broken in every part

Even in death He thought of me
Knowing without Him I could not be
In what sounded like His final breath
He entrusted me to John upon His death
I knew His Father's heart was also broken
For heaven cried and the earth was shaken

That night I lay sleepless upon my bed
For when I close my eyes, I saw my baby—dead!
Blood flowing freely from His hands and feet
From nine-inches spikes, driven down deep

I buried my child in a borrowed tomb
And with these hands, I anointed His wounds
I remembered what the olden prophets foretold
That this child would bring both joy and sorrow to my soul

Joy upon the night when I laid Him in the manger
And angels proclaimed that my baby was the Savior
Sorrow upon this day that He gave grace
To save the entire human race
His disciples scattered far and wide
When once upon a time, they were all by His side

But on the third day, the Father cried:
Jesus! My Son! Arise!
And the earth quaked
And the stone rolled away
And Jesus stepped forth the resurrection and the way

So you see why He's my awesome child
My lowly Jesus, meek and mild
The King of kings, once my baby
It takes faith to believe it really

And now He's in heaven to reign as King
An advocate if you or I sin
And though He sits upon His throne
He's yearning to come and take me home

He's my awesome Child
He's God's Son but He's also mine

Before Word

Miracles Birthed from Barren and Virgin Wombs

*T*here they were on the brink of changing the course of humanity's eternal destiny—linked by familial bond and a singular purpose. Cousins, born mere three months apart, one to proclaim the arrival of the Savior and one to be the Savior.

There they were standing at the threshold bridging the Old and the New Testaments, at the intersection of Savior promised and Savior born—a forerunner and a Savior, John the Baptizer and Jesus the Messiah.

The inspiration for *"Salvation's Price"*, the next poetic expression, came after reflecting on the way the lives of John and Jesus intersected; and how clear and resolute they both were about their purpose. Even before he was born, John responded to his calling—at six-months old he leapt for joy within his mother's womb upon hearing the voice of Mary who was at the time in the first month of her pregnancy with Jesus. (Saint Luke 1:41)

And when the time came for Jesus to take up His role as Savior, John acknowledged that his role as Forerunner was complete and ushered his followers to Jesus with these prophesy-fulfilling words: *"Behold the Lamb of God"* (Saint John 1:36, King James Version) and willingly faded from the limelight. (Saint John 3:30)

Oh to be so dogged in purpose even knowing the full extent of the cost of its attainment, *"Salvation's Price"*.

SALVATION'S PRICE

29 December 1998

Part I

John, did you really understand
The full extent of redemption's plan?

What honour you must have felt
When the Saviour before you knelt?

I must decrease so He may increase
With that submission, your ministry ceased

Part II

Jesus, what thoughts through Your mind raced
Knowing there was a Gethsemane and a Calvary to face?

Though rich, You became poor
Emptied Yourself in order to restore

The Son of God, the ultimate sacrifice
Only supreme love could pay the price

You gave up Your sceptre, from Your throne stepped down
Knowing You'd be rejected, mistreated, spat upon

Could You see through the portals of the grave?
Were you assured the Father would accept the sacrifice You gave?

And when Your Father turned His face away
Could Yu foresee the victory of the third day?

Were You scared You had paid too high a price for man's
    redemption?
Did You see Yourself coming forth a conqueror over sin's
    condemnation?

Part III

At every cost, John offered all
Invitation extended to heed the call

Mankind's redemption in Jesus complete
Condemnation from sin lay in defeat

Salvation bought at the highest price
The lives of John the Forerunner and the Saviour, Jesus Christ

Before Word

The Miracle of God Becoming Man

I was born into Christianity and attended church because my mother and later my aunt made sure I did. It was only after I migrated to Canada, away from their influence, that I questioned whether their beliefs were also my own. This forced me into researching Christianity and other religions.

One of the elements of Christianity that helped me embrace it as my own belief system was the nature of God; and more specifically, that God became man.

I was awed that God—the Almighty—would become man; and that He sacrificed Himself in order to redeem a rebellious race. And in becoming human, He did not come as an adult but as a baby so that He could experience all the nuances of life as I do; that He could be tempted in all the areas as I am tempted; that He could experience love and hate and loss and gains; and, to cry and laugh in the same way I do. In order to be fully acquainted with the feelings of my infirmities, He lived life on earth as an example for me.

THIS FORMS THE BASIS OF MY FAITH!

I know there is nothing I will face that He did not face and overcame. And, I therefore have the assurance that if He overcame, so can I. (Hebrews 4:14-15)

And throughout the ages He will forever be associated with humanity—He will always bear the scar in His hands and feet, the symbols that entitles Him to be *"The God-Man"*.

Jehovah God—Elohim, El-Shaddai, Adonai, Nissi, Rohi, Jireh, Rapha, Raah—I choose You! And I will choose You over and over and over again!

Dawn A. Minott

THE GOD-MAN

4 February 1999

Phase I: His Birth

Do you know the God who became a fetus
Wrapped up in a virgin's womb to save us?

Gave up His throne and royal crown
From heavenly portals He stepped down

Born in a place not fit for a King
Only shepherds heard the angels sing

With donkeys and horses, in a lowly manger on hay
A helpless child in Mary's arms lay

Herod tried to have Him slain
To stop the purpose for which He came

A humble birth to fulfill salvation's plan
Born into humanity God became man

Phase II: His Life

Do you know the Man, who is part of the Godhead
But thought it not robbery to become man instead?

The Man who worked miracles untold
Interested always in the salvation of souls

He healed the sick and raised the dead
And from His presence demons fled

He touched the bones and the crippled walked
Spoke to the dumb and straightway they talked

Mothers brought their children to Him
For healing from the maladies within

Never before had they seen such a Man
And not thereafter, for He is the only One

Phase III: His Death

Do you know the Man who chose the cross
Sacrificing His life to pay sin's ultimate cost?

In the Garden of Gethsemane burdened with strife
The weight of all humanity's sins crushing out His life

He yearned for human sympathy amidst intense affliction
His disciples slept, unaware of His pending crucifixion

Alone He wrestled the powers of darkness
On bended knees embraced only by nature's caress

Three times His lips released the feverish cry:
From Me let this pass Father, but Your will I won't deny

Then down the Via Dolorosa, up to Calvary to face
Death upon a rugged cross to save the human race

Phase IV: His Glory

Do you know the Man, who ascended to Glory
To complete the mystery of redemption's story?

Three days He slept in the hollow of the grave
His tomb guarded by soldiers steadfast and brave

Hosts of evil angels gathered there to see
That His resurrection would not come to be

Heaven's messenger rolled the stone away
Jesus came forth without delay

In heaven now seated on His throne
Preparing to return and take home His own

Only those who've accepted salvation's plan
Only those who truly know the God-Man

Before Word

The Miracle Coalesced in Mercy, Grace and Love

*T*hat God would choose to make the ultimate sacrifice to save humanity though He foreknew that all humanity would not accept His sacrifice is the amalgamation of mercy, grace and love.

The miracle coalesced in mercy, grace and love is best exemplified in the Biblical story of a woman caught in the act of adultery. (Saint John 8:4) This story appears in only one of the four Gospels—the book of Saint John. Though there has been much debate about its authorship and its authenticity as part of the life of Christ, I find it to be one of the best examples of mercy, grace and love.

I was intrigued by this story first because it showed that Jesus was intolerant of 'isms' such as male chauvinism and sexism. Being "caught in the act" implies that both the woman and the man were present. However, it was the woman alone who was brought before Jesus for condemnation even though the Law of Moses stipulated that both the man and the woman should be put to death (Leviticus 20:10).

The second thing that intrigued me about this story is the fact that Jesus used His fingers to write in the dust. You may be wondering what the intrigue is.

Well, there are only three recorded times in the Bible that God used His fingers to write—once when He wrote the Ten Commandments setting forth His standard of righteousness as a mirror for humankind to see their sinfulness (Exodus 31:18); and the second time when He gave a message of judgment to King Belshazzar (Daniel 5:5). Both times He wrote on stone—**concreted matter.**

Inscriptions in stone imply permanence.

The third time God wrote with His fingers was in the story of the woman caught in the act of adultery. However, on this occasion He wrote in the **dust**. This tells us that not only will God show up in the dirtiness of our sins, but He'll acknowledge them in **dust—tiny particles that are easily scattered and dissipated.**

Inscriptions in dust are not meant to be permanent.

Like dust, so are our sins removed, scattered as far as the east is from the west. That is mercy, grace and love coalesced to save us and that is the intrigue!

My meditation on how mercy, grace and love converged in this story influenced the next poem, *"No Accusers"*.

Dawn A. Minott

NO ACCUSERS

8 September 1997

I was caught in the act, but dragged in alone
For the men couldn't see the wrong in one of their own
Ashamed for I knew the crowd spoke the truth
Annoyed for society would not condemn him too
Body hunched, head bowed, eyes transfixed to the ground
I waited in fear the fate I expected His voice would sound

Stooping all the way down to my level He slowly wrote
With His fingers in the dirt not once looking about
Omniscient revelation, my accusers' sins made known
Thoughts and actions once hidden now shown
His exposure would not allow them to slay
One by one they hurriedly slithered away

"Woman, where are your accusers?" He enquired
Though He already knew all that had transpired
Alas—I looked up, there was no one in sight
Not an accuser or accomplice, only One who understood my plight
Hugging Him I exhaled in bitter-sweet relief
A cry of gratitude for I was granted full reprieve

"No accusers Lord! No one left here but You and me!"
"You are forgiven, go now, live unto Me a life sin-free"
In that moment I knew I'd sin no more
For in Him my self-worth was fully restored
No need to hop from bed to bed
My bewildered spirit was finally fed

What accusers have you encountered?
Who've marred your name or brought you shame?
Who've dragged you before a disciplinary board?
Expecting condemnation to settle the score?
Can you see Jesus stooping, getting down to your level?
Hear Him say: My child, go now, your sins are forgiven
Then with rejoicing you too will say
No accusers Lord
None left here but me and You

Before Word

The Miracle of Grace

*W*hen I wanted to find a life that exemplified the miracle that is grace, I looked to the lives recorded in the Bible. And, when I wanted to find an example of how to apply grace to my own life, the practicality of the Psalmist David drew me to his life record. More specifically, the record of the time he disobeyed God and numbered the Israelites. God rebuked David for his disobedience through the prophet Gad. In His rebuke, God gave David his choice of chastisement (1 Chronicles 21: 11-13):

1) 3 months defeat at the hand of their enemies;
2) 3 years famine; or
3) 3 days at the hand of the Lord.

David, understanding the grace of God, was deliberate in his response:

> *". . . I am in great distress. Please let me fall into the hand of the Lord, for His mercies are very great; but do not let me fall into the hand of man."* (1 Chronicles 21:13 New King James Version)

You may be quick to reason that David chose chastisement at the hand of the Lord because it was only for three days compared to three months or three years. But that is where you would miss the miracle that is grace.

You see, David knew first-hand about human passion and vengeance—he knew they had no bounds. He had been hounded mercilessly for years by a troubled king, King Saul. Juxtaposed to that experience, David knew that God in His gracious-kindness and wisdom meets out just the right amount of what is needed to not only chastise but to redeem; and, that it is done in and with love, not vengeance or hate.

We can rest assured that at the point where God first graciously meets us is where we can expect to meet Him again and again. We may stray, but He won't move away from the **point of grace**.

GRACE is the manifestation of God as the
supreme Poet recreating us into
His *poiema,*
His masterpiece,
His work of art.

Grace is freely bestowed, it does not have to be earned or repaid. Grace is purely the work of God alone in seeking and saving. Human works have no part in it. In fact, if our works or our self-efforts to be righteous are involved, then grace ceases to be grace. For grace is not tantamount to our dos or don'ts, grace is simply God's work complete in our SALVATION!

GRACE:
God's **R**ighteousness **A**t **C**hrist's **E**xpense

GOD'S RIGHTEOUSNESS AT CHRIST'S EXPENSE

October 7, 2011

The Bride: Rebellion

Dressed me in a spotless robe of white
Covenanted Your love and favor
Wowed to be forever mine
Placed Your symbol on my heart, Your ring of love
Though I have not chosen You
You chose me as Your bride
Called me Your betrothed

You know all my iniquities
Heard each harsh word I have spoken
Perceived each sinful intent
Seen each act of vindication
Know my thoughts before they're conceived
Yet You lavish Your love upon me freely
Called me Your espoused

What will it take for You to leave me?
Not be jealous over me?
One more lover?
One more heartbreak?
One more prodigal mistake?
Don't you see my nature's against You?
What I desire I do not do
It's my natural inclination
I will turn again from You

Once more I have betrayed You
Once more helplessly enslaved
On the auction block I'm standing
Not worth more than Your reproach
One more time You've bid with everything
Gave your life to emancipate mine
How is it that You still love me?
Arms stretched outward to embrace me
Draped in a robe once spotless white
Now drenched with stains of trespasses and sins

The Groom: Restoration

Here I stand in love and mercy
Giving all to gain you back
Returning you from a past that needs forgetting
Repairing the separation that needs bridging
Restoring a mind that needs renewing
Replacing the emptiness that needs fulfilling
Redeeming a nature that needs transforming
Reconciling a heart that needs forgiving

Again I give my gift of GRACE
Abundantly lavished upon you by Me

It has always been my GRACE
Stubbornly maintaining you through Me

It will always be by GRACE
Irresistibly drawing you to Me

It is only through GRACE
Intently securing you with Me

It will for always be GRACE
Triumphantly exclaiming you're forever Mine

The Bride & Groom: Consummation

> Restored like I had never sinned?
>> All's forgiven and forgotten
>
> I am Yours and You are mine?
>> Covered again in My robe of white
>
> Covenanted again with Your ring?
>> Know I will love you always
>
> Will You ask again the question?
>> Will you be forever mine?
>
> Yes, I accept You as my Husband
>> You are now forever Mine
>
> Place Your ring upon my heart
>> You're My church, My betrothed, My bride

Before Word

The Miracle of Salvation & the Gift of Eternal Life

*C*he experience that inspired the composition of *"The Dream"* remains one of the most defining and poignant moments in my growing to know the heart of God.

This experience came very early in my Christian experience—a dash-like moment betwixt and between my understanding and acceptance of the assurance of salvation. It was at the point where I had busied myself serving in the church, but had not spent the time needed to get to know God. Now I understand that God calls us into relationship, not church; and, it is out of this relationship that we serve. Lacking this understanding, however, meant I did not have the assurance in *knowing* I was saved, and it is in this context I prayed asking God if I was saved. Knowing what I know now, it was a ludicrous prayer because all I had to do was accept the gift of salvation and in the faith of Jesus know that I am saved. God, being God, however answered my prayer—that very night I dreamt I was lost.

I am not in any way implying that it is God's intent that I, or any other, should be lost. In fact, He says that it is His **patient desire** that **ALL** should come to repentance (2 Peter 3:9). What the dream did do, however, was to serve as the wake-up call I needed which turned me on to a better understanding

**The Good News
of SALVATION is this:**

Through the death of Jesus, God forever united the divinity of Jesus with our humanity in order to redeem us. In other words, when God looks at us He sees us clothed in the righteousness of His Son—redeemed. Our part is simply to accept Jesus' righteousness by faith; to identify ourselves with His life, death and resurrection and to be obedient to the word of God.

of the gospel as the GOOD NEWS OF SALVATION, and started me on this quest to know the heart of God.

The Good News of SALVATION (continues)

So, the <u>A-B-C</u> of it is this: you <u>A</u>ccept that Jesus is the Son of God; you <u>B</u>elieve that there is no other way to be saved but through Jesus; and you <u>C</u>ommit to living your life to please Him. If you make the decision to follow Jesus and you declare it (or confess with your mouth), God accepts you and in that very MOMENT you are saved!

This, however, does not give you license to live as you please. Instead, it gives you access to the righteousness of Christ so that you can be empowered to live for Him and grow in His grace.

The amazing and mysterious transfer that took place with the sacrifice of Jesus is this: Jesus was made to be sin for humanity in order that humanity might become the righteousness of God in Him (2 Corinthians 5:21).

The first time I came to understand this, not just read it but comprehend what it really meant, it made me say aloud:

"What? God is some kind o' crazy!"

That was a gigantic, humongous gamble to take on me when He knew my beginning, my in-between and my end. Yet, in spite of all He knew He made Jesus become sin for me on the off-chance that I would accept the sacrifice and become His righteousness in Jesus. And, to top it all off, He goes about reciting me/His *poiema* to anyone who would listen.

There is a whole bandstand in heaven—what the Bible calls "a GREAT cloud of witnesses" (Hebrews 12:1)—all witnessing God brag on me. Oh yeah, that is some kind o' crazy! If I don't love Him for anything else, I love Him because He's crazy in love with me.

Every believing sinner has been made the righteousness of God!

Isn't that good news?

As you journey to the heart of God, you may miss the mark or a "peg" or two of your "fruit" may be smaller than they should be. But, if you remain faithful in seeking after God, eventually your heart will begin to line up to His heart and in time your heart will look like God's. And without even realizing the process, one day you'll look at yourself and ask: *"When did I stop doing this thing and that thing?"* That is when you will know and fully understand that you are now established in the righteousness of God.

When you're established in His righteousness you will not want to do the things that are unlike Him. So you see, God's graciousness toward us is not a license to sin but as we come to the realization that we are the righteousness of God, we can come to God knowing that He loves us and will not hold our sins against us. In imputing or accrediting His righteousness through Christ, God made it possible for the sins of the believing sinner to be atoned for—that is, sins past and sins to come—so that we can be reconciled to God. I don't know about you, but I am totally awed by that!

Going back to the premise laid out in the Introduction, I reiterate—we can in deed live every day. But, by choosing salvation in this life it takes every-day living a step further to establish our access to eternal life. This begs the question though—if we have access to eternal life, do we truly only die once? Or, is there also eternal death? God says,

> *"For surely there is a hereafter . . . ."* (Proverbs 23:18, New King James Version)

> *"This day I call the heavens and the earth as witnesses against you that I have set before you life and death . . . . Now choose life, so that you . . . may live".* (Deuteronomy 30:19, New International Version).

The choice is ours. In fact, there is only one choice. God beckons us to choose life; that is, eternal life and if not then we by default have chosen death, eternal death. As it is possible to have the abundant life and gain eternal life, so it is possible to die more than once, the second being the eternal death.

"The Dream" is based on my dream-experience of being eternally lost and faced with eternal death; but, it does not have to be your lived-reality. Salvation is a gift; therefore, there is nothing you have to do to attain it except to accept it. It will not be forced upon you—it is yours for the choosing and the receiving.

THE DREAM

16 December 2003

'Twas the night before Jesus returned
And all through the universe, not a sound was heard
Not a creature stirred, not even a mouse
And there was half-an-hour's silence in the Father's house

My children reluctantly crawled into bed
As I tucked them in snugly with a kiss on each head
No one said a prayer, and no one was aware
That the second coming of the King was awfully near

I sat on the sofa, exhausted and tired
But my favorite 'Soap' I must watch before I retire
As soon as it's finished, I'll read the Bible
And say a quick prayer, if I'm still able

When out from the east arose such a clatter
I sprang to my feet to see what was the matter
I raced to the window in a lightning flash
Tore open the louvers, and lifted the sash

When what to my wondering eyes should appear . . .
But thousands of angels proclaiming: "Jesus is here!"
Jesus is here?
In spite of myself I ran away and hid
I was not prepared. "Jesus, did I let go of that one small sin?"

Jesus turned the pages of the Book of Life held in His hand
With a thundering voice, He called the name of every saved one
Now Mary . . . now Joseph . . . now Ruth . . . where's Esther?
And David . . . and Dorcas . . . come on John . . . where's Peter?

No . . . that can't all be
You still haven't called me
I cried, and wept, and pleaded with Him
Look again—please—my name must be within

I looked into His eyes, how they narrowed with pain and sorrow
As His nail-pierced hand pointed me to my darkest tomorrow
"Depart from me, I know you not" I heard Him sadly say
There was no more time to say: "forgive me", I turned and slowly
walked away

Then I saw the children of darkness running to and fro
To hide from Him seated upon the majestic throne
Their horrid screams penetrated the hollow night
They were caught in a dreadful, inescapable fright

Had I not been told, I would not believe
The looming, ghastly and frightful scene
The whole earth began to heave and shake
Great mountains moved by a mighty quake

The bowels of the sea moaned and groaned
Sending shivers to an already petrified crowd
Yet the children of darkness cursed their plight
As one by one, they were slain by His radiant light

They slept engulfed in death's deep slumber
Undisturbed by the trumpets and a voice so tender
It was the voice of Jesus as He summoned the just
"Awake! Arise My children! Time to shake off the dust"

Into their tombs glorious beams find their way
Awaking each with a gentle touch and a sway
And one by one they came up from the grave
Standing face to face with their Savior of Grace

As quickly as a wink they were all changed
Up . . . up . . . and away, they swiftly flew out of range
Then I heard Jesus exclaimed ere He rose out of sight:
"I'm taking My children home where there'll be no more night?"

His children—His children did not include me
Though I served the "church" faithfully
Now my soul's eternally lost
I had squandered the gift He gave on the cross

I cried in despair as Christ disappeared from my sight
If only I knew this would have been the night
I would have let go of my earthly possessions
And brought before the Lord all my sins in confession

If nothing else from this poem fell on your ear
Believe me when I tell you Jesus' coming is quite near
NOW is the time for you to walk in His way
Not sooner or later, but right now—today!

Though this was a dream, soon it will be
The day when Jesus' return we'll see
Repentance then will be too late
Won't you enter now through mercy's gate?

Before Word

𝒯he time it took to prepare this book for publication spanned 2011 and 2012 and with the passing of each month it seemed the ferociousness of natural disasters and the heinousness of humanity's evil actions intensified.

- Citizens from Tunisia, Egypt, Syria, and Libya revolted leading to long-time dictators ousted or killed and a tragic human toll of suffering, bloodshed and loss of life.
- A 9.0 magnitude earthquake hit Japan, shifted the earth off its axis, triggered a tsunami and nuclear disaster leaving 15,843 dead, 3,469 missing, 5,890 injured and over 300,000 displaced.
- A storm so catastrophic it was dubbed the "Frankenstorm" caused unprecedented flooding in the North-East corridor of the United States changing forever the coastal landscape, decimating thousands of households, claiming over 100 lives, crippling transportation, and plunged the "city that never sleeps" (New York) into death-like stillness and darkness.
- Home-grown terrorism obliterated the lives of over 70 people in a bomb-and-shooting massacre in Norway.
- And, the most horrific of all, in the United States after a series of mass-shootings each getting more vehement than the other, assault rifles were mercilessly unleashed on 20 children all under the age of 6 years along with 6 adults slaughtering them in one of the places they should be the safest—their school.

And, amidst these disasters and evil acts we've each experienced individual trauma enough for us to want to be in a better time and a better place. However, if what the Bible prophesies is true, and I believe that it is, then a better time and place will not be on this earth.

God has promised *"a new heaven and a new earth"*. (Revelation 21:1) However, believing in a new heaven and a new earth means one must first believe in the God who made this promise. Yet there are many who do not believe that God exists. A paper from the Cambridge Companion to Atheism, *"Atheism: Contemporary Rates and Patterns"*, confirms this reality across a number of countries. For example, 30 per cent of Canadians do not believe in God or a higher power; while that number stands at 54 per cent for Swedes and 61 per cent for Czechs.

Based on this reality, it seems to me the Christian philosopher, Blaise Pascal, got it right when he posited that: if there is a wager that "God is" or "God is not" to bet that "God is" and win is to gain all; that is, an infinity of an infinitely happy life. And, if you lose, you lose nothing. However, if you wager that "God is not" and "God is", then you gain nothing and lose everything.

This journey to getting to know the heart of God has reinforced my resolve—I believe in God. My wager has been and will continue to be: "God is"! And whatever it costs for this belief, it will all be worth it to hear my heavenly Father say just two words: **"Well Done!"**

Dawn A. Minott

WELL DONE

27 August 2010

Heartbeat racing
Life's turmoil winds blowing
Depression's darkness engulfing
Forsaken, rejected, tears cascading
No end in sight, faith unraveling

Hold on, be strong, morning's breaking
Weeping endures for just the night
Joy will come in the morning light

Heartaches come but they won't last
Sorrow's pain in the distant past
Don't let go, keep holding on
You'll make it through, just you stay strong

All around the signs are telling
Scientists fail in their explaining
Earthquakes shaking, winds enraging
From its core the earth's erupting
Stars falling, landscapes flooding

Rejoice in knowing He is coming
To usher in the grand homecoming
Where there'll be no more heartbreaking

All I have, that's what I'll give
My love, my heart, this life I live
My song, my dance, my music, my voice
All testify, I've made Him my choice

I know one day He'll crack the sky
I'll bid this sorrowful world goodbye
It will be worth it when He comes
To hear Him say:
"My child, well done!"

Nevertheless, Afterward

> *"His lord said unto him, well done, good and faithful servant: enter thou into the joy of thy Lord."* (Saint Matthew 25:23, King James Version)

My Heart-Poem to God

Daddy,

You've done all that could possibly be done to show me that You love me. You've done all that could possibly be done in order to save me. For all I've been through, and all that is to come, it will be worth it all just to hear You say, "Welcome home My child, well done!"

My whole life I've heard it said: "Jesus is coming soon". Father, whether it happens in my lifetime or not, my only desire is to be a part of the faithful throng, that host that no one could number, who will spend eternity with You.

Father, 'til that day keep me faithful to You. And if for any reason my will is not aligned to Yours, please make me willing to be willing to You always.

I love You! Can't wait to see You!

For always, Your child
Dawn Angela Minott

Your Heart-Poem to God

Dear Reader,

Use the space below to share with God your thoughts on Jesus returning to earth a second time whether it may seem mythical to you or very real. Open your heart to receive His response.

CHAPTER 6

HEART-TO-HEART

The Heart of God

*W*hen I first shared the objective of this book with a friend, that of documenting my heart-moments in journeying to the heart of God, he asked: *what is the heart of God?*

If you decide you will race through the next few sentences to get to the definition of God's heart as I shared it with my friend, let me hasten to apologize because I cannot definitively say what the heart of God is. What I will share with you is my understanding of God's heart as I'm getting to know Him from which you may draw your own conclusion as you are on your quest to also know His heart.

When you and I speak about the "heart" we refer to the seat of our emotions and feelings. However, as I am on this life-changing journey I'm growing to understand that the heart of God refers to more than the emotions and feelings of God. And yes, God has emotions and feelings—He laughs and He cries; He sings over us and even gets jealous over us; He also gets angry; and, He experiences sorrow.

I am learning that:

**Knowing the heart of God means
going beyond seeing the hand of God.**

What I mean is this—we tend to base our knowledge of people by what they do and we extend that same standard to gauge our knowledge of God. However, **if I am unable to extend my knowledge of God to more than just His "doing", then my faith in Him will wane when He is not "doing" or when He is silent.**

It is true that I am comforted in the knowledge of who God is by what He does or when He demonstrates His power in my life. However, this does not mean I know Him intimately or that I'm tight with Him. Why? Because His "doing" cannot be used as an indicator to measure relationship or fellowship since He liberally extends His "doing", such as providing sunshine and rainfall, equally to the righteous and the unrighteous (Saint Matthew 5:45).

This is why it is not sufficient, though necessary, to be grateful for the doings of His hand; but, to move beyond gratitude to knowing His heart.

To have a HEART-TO-HEART relationship with God means acquainting myself with the deepest recesses of His being—of who He IS. And who is God? Well, He tells us in His word:

*"Whoever does not love does not know God, because **God is love"***. (1 John 4:8, New International Version)

GOD IS LOVE!
LOVE IS GOD!
Therefore
The HEART of God is LOVE!

The love that is of God is a sacrificial love; it's a self-giving love. It is a love that is independent of the worthiness of the object upon which it is bestowed. It is a love that keeps on loving even when love is not returned. It is a love that will not die. Though I cannot love in this perfect way, it is God's intent to teach how to love Him in this way so I can in turn love others.

How can I learn this kind of love? In one of His poetic expressions, Jesus explained the means through which we can attain this kind of love. He said:

> *"As the Father loved Me, I also have loved you;* **abide** *in My love. If you keep My commandments, You will* **abide** *in My love, just as I have kept My Father's commandments and* **abide** *in His love."*
> (Saint John 15:9-10, New King James Version)

Three times in one sentence Jesus uses "abide". What Jesus is emphasizing is relationship. And not just any type of relationship but one that is intimate and tight, one that is based on abiding and obedience.

Abiding is spending meaningful time with God. This includes:

- *Dwelling in His presence*—this could take various forms such as quiet time in worship and praise or gathering with fellow believers;
- *Talking to Him as you talk to a friend*—such as giving thanks, making your requests known, interceding for someone else, seeking forgiveness;
- *Reading His Word*—not as a habit but as a means of getting to know Him; searching for those little nuggets that will give you insights into who He is; and,
- *Meditating on His Word*—applying what you've read to situations in your life, or in other words making a life-application from the Word.

And most importantly, it is necessary to be **obedient** to His will, to whatever He reveals to you.

Now you're on your way to knowing the heart of God. In time you will see a change in you and will have the satisfaction of hearing God testify of you:

_____'s heart looks like My heart".
(Insert your name)

CONCLUSION

$\mathcal{T}$hroughout this book I sought to share a selection of heart-moments from my life journey to know the heart of God, and how my relationship with Him is enabling me to not only live life but to have life and to have it more abundantly.

I started off this journey by arguing that life is but a collection of moments, and that each moment should be lived to the fullest in order to attain a meaningful life. This argument was made on the reality that life is temporary—it spans birth to death—it is merely our physical existence. To live this physical life is to exist, to be in this world, or simply to breathe. At the cessation of your moments when you cease to exist or to breathe, death has found you; and in that moment, your physical life ceases to exist and all you attained will over time fritter away.

On the contrary, the Bible extends this physical existence to include a spiritual component, or spiritual life, which is attainable through a relationship with Jesus Christ. This is what Jesus offers. He says:

> *"I am come that [you] may <u>have</u> life, and . . . have it more abundantly".* (Saint John 10:10, New King James Version)

Notice Jesus' invitation is first to HAVE life. To HAVE is to own, possess, enjoy or exhibit. In other words, He's offering Himself because *"in Him was life"* (Saint John 1:4); which is not an ordinary existence, but life in its fullest. So, in accepting Jesus we HAVE (own, possess, enjoy, exhibit) His life and this is not temporary or ordinary.

Secondly, Jesus' invitation is to have life more abundantly. According to the Blue Letter Bible, the word "abundantly" comes from the Greek word *"perissos"* which means *"exceeding some number or measure or rank or need; something further, more, much more than all; and over and above, more than is necessary, superadded".* What could exceed life? Only life-everlasting or –eternal, or life that is not temporary or ordinary; and this is the life Jesus is calling us into.

Anyone who accepts this invitation to receive Jesus will by extension receive the abundant life because it is an inherent part of who He is. The abundant life is one that is based on ongoing fellowship with God and all the benefits that stem from that, the ultimate being eternal life.

Having life more abundantly is not to be confused with material abundance—the primary purpose of Jesus's mission was not so I can have an abundance of material possessions but that I can have an abundance of spiritual blessings which will enable me to HAVE the abundant life and ultimately God's gift—eternal life.

As I am on this journey to know the heart of God I am learning **how to move from LIVING the ordinary life to HAVING the abundant life.**

- First, I ***cannot live in the past***. To HAVE life is to be in Christ because in Him is life.

   "Therefore, if anyone is in Christ, he is a new creation; old things have passed away; behold, all things have become new." (2 Corinthians 5:17, New King James Version)

   So if I'm in Christ, I'm a new creature and I must live in that reality. I use my past as a point of reference, but I don't dwell there. Instead, I keep pressing forward toward the mark which is the ultimate prize—the high calling of God in Christ Jesus. (Philippians 3:14)

- Second, *I must believe that abundant life is God's highest desire for me*. It's the only reason why Jesus came.

  "I am come that [you] may have life, and . . . have it more abundantly". (Saint John 10:10, New King James Version)

I am humbled by knowing that God, the Almighty, loves me so much that not only does His grace seek after me, but it also saves me. God chases after me, He pursues me. Why? So He can win my heart and lavish on me this amazing gift that I may in turn enjoy abundant life in Him. Every time I think of the depth of God's love for me, I am awestruck.

- And, third, I have to *align my highest desire with God's*. God has done everything He can do so I may have abundant life but He will not force it on me. He says,

  Here I am! I stand at the door and knock. If anyone hears my voice and opens the door, I will come in and eat with him, and he with me." (Revelation 3:20, New International Version)

Even though God knows abundant life is His highest desire for me, I must choose to accept it as the highest desire for myself. When I do, then He'll come into fellowship with me. This tells me that above everything else, **God just wants me to want Him**.

The realness of what this means impacted me after I fell in love with someone who did not feel the same way about me. Of all the things I desired during that phase of my life, I remember my strongest yearning was for him to want me. Knowing that he did not, I felt dejected. Conversely, here is God inviting me into relationship and fellowship with

Him—offering me the purest, truest love—and I reject Him and His love. Does He also feel dejected?

After all God has done for me, the thought that my actions could cause Him any kind of grief drives me to want to want Him; and, in so doing to be the recipient of His love, His fellowship and His abundant life. And, unlike giving my affections to someone who may not reciprocate, I have nothing to lose with God because He already loves me; in fact, He loved me before I even knew Him.

So, when all I can say has been said, and all I can do has been done, and death finds me at the cessation of my moments, I hope it finds me content in knowing that I lived every MOMENT like it was my last; comforted that my life-journey ended at the heart of God; and, confident that I have Jesus and therefore have life more abundantly, the everlasting life.

AFTERWORD

Dear Reader,

In welcoming you to this book, I invited you to make this your journey to the heart of God as well. So, it would be remiss of me to end this book and not provide the space for you to make or renew your commitment to journey to the heart of God.

You now know that you too can have abundant life and that there is nothing you have to do, or in deed nothing you can do, to earn it. You simply accept it for what it is, a gift. What does this mean? It's simple really—if you confess those times when you have been deliberately disobedient to the expressed will of God (what is summarized as sins); if you acknowledge that there is nothing you can do to rid yourself of sin; and let God know that you accept His gift to cover your sin in the form of Jesus, then you ARE saved.

If that is your desire, pray this simple prayer and believe:

> Dear God,
>
> I recognize that I am a sinner.
> I believe that Jesus is the Son of God and that through His death I am forgiven and saved.
> Come into my life now and help me to live for You.
>
> Amen

God has accepted you. You are saved!

If you could but get a glimpse in the throne room of God right now, you would be mesmerized by the intensity of praise that is taking place. Why? Well, because all of Heaven has this magnificent practice of bursting into rapturous rejoicing over one person who repents and commits his or her life to God. (Saint Luke 15:7) Smile! You are the cause for Heaven's current jubilation and exuberance!

I would love to share in your heart journey to the heart of God. Drop me a line at moments@dawnminott.com.

If you've just given your heart to God, or renewed your commitment to Him, use the space below to thank Him for His gift of grace and eternal life. If you are still undecided, let Him know what delays you in accepting His gift and prepare your heart to receive His response.

_____

_____

_____

_____

_____

_____

_____

_____

_____

Journey's End

The Heart of God

ABOUT THE AUTHOR

Dawn A. Minott was born in Jamaica where she grew up with her mother and her maternal aunt. After migrating to Canada to live with her father, she attended York University. She holds a BA and MA in Political Science, with a concentration in International Relations and Comparative Politics, as well as a specialized Certificate in Refugee & Migration Studies. And, she is now pursuing a degree in "Interior Design".

Dawn currently lives in New York and works for the United Nations. As an International Civil Servant, she has travelled extensively, and has done assignments in her home country Jamaica, as well as in Barbados, South Africa, Nigeria, and the Headquarters in New York.

Dawn's greatest satisfaction comes from being a Christian and an ambassador for God. She has served in various capacities in her church, working especially with young people and women. Her ultimate goal is to be able to make a difference in the lives of all those she's been privileged to come into contact with.

Dawn is a prolific writer and motivational speaker. She has preached to church congregations in Barbados, South Africa and the United States, and made presentations to young people and women in various fora. Dawn has published in magazines and newspapers on issues ranging from engendering democracy to ending violence against women, reproductive health and HIV/AIDS. Pieces of her poetic work are also available in *"Our Words, Our Revolutions"* (Inanna Publications & Education Inc., Canada, 2000).

REFERENCES

Babatunde Olatunji. (n.d.). Retrieved December 10, 2011, from BrainyQuote.com, website: http://www.brainyquote.com/quotes/authors/b/babatunde_olatunji.html

Barnstone, Willis. *"Jesus Christ the Invisible Poet in the Gospels."* The Poems of Jesus Christ. W. W. Norton & Company: New York, London. 2012. Page xv.

Blue Letter Bible. *"Dictionary and Word Search for "perissos" (Strong's 4053)"*. 1996-2012. 5 November 2012. http://www.blueletterbible.org/lang/lexicon/Lexicon.cfm?Strongs=G4053&cscs=Phl

Cowman, Charles E. Streams in the Dessert, Zondervan Publishing House, Michigan, USA. 1965.

Leo Tolstoy. (n.d.). Retrieved December 10, 2011, from BrainyQuote.com, website: http://www.brainyquote.com/quotes/quotes/l/leotolstoy132395.html

"Miracle". Retrieved November 12, 2011 from http://oxforddictionaries.com/definition/english/miracle

"Pascal's Wager". Retrieved December 20, 2012 from http://en.wikipedia.org/wiki/Pascal's_Wager

Zuckerman, Phil. *Atheism: Contemporary Rates and Patterns* from the Cambridge Companion to Atheism. Michael Martin, Editor, University of Cambridge Press, 2007.

Bible References (in order of appearance)

1. *"Now no chastening for the present seems to be joyous, but grievous; nevertheless, afterward it yields the peaceable fruit of righteousness unto them which are exercised thereby."* (Hebrews 12:11, King James Version)

2. *"And God said, let there be light; and there was light."* (Genesis 1:3, King James Version)

3. *"For the invisible things of Him from the creation of the world are clearly seen, being understood by the things that are made, even His eternal power and Godhead; so that they are without excuse."* (Romans 1:20, King James Version)

4. *"For we are His workmanship, created in Christ Jesus unto good works, which God hath before ordained that we should walk in them."* (Ephesians 2:10, King James Version)

5. *"Look at the lilies in the field and how they grow they don't work or make their clothing yet Solomon in all his glory was not dressed as beautifully as they are. And if God cares so wonderfully for wildflowers that are here today and thrown into the fire tomorrow He will certainly care for you."* (Saint Matthew 6:28-30, Life Application Study Bible)

6. *"If ye shall ask anything in My name, I will do it."* (Saint John 14:14, King James Version)

7. *"Look at the birds of the air for they neither sow nor reap nor gather into barns yet their heavenly Father feeds them are you not of more value than they?"* (Saint Matthew 6:26, New King James Version)

8. *"A man's heart plans his way, but the Lord directs his steps."* (Proverbs 16:9, New King James Version)

9. *"There are many plans in a man's heart, nevertheless the Lord's counsel that will stand."* (Proverbs 19:21, New King James Version)

10. *"And I will add unto thy days fifteen years; and I will deliver thee and this city out of the hand of the king of Assyria; and I will defend this city for Mine own sake, and for My servant David's sake."* (2 Kings 20:6, King James Version)

11. *"And you fathers, do not provoke your children to anger, but bring them up in the discipline and instruction of the Lord."* (Ephesians 6:4, English Standard Version)

12. *"God sets the solitary in families; He brings out those who are bound into prosperity; but the rebellious dwell in a dry land."* (Psalm 68:5, New King James Version)

13. *"A father to the fatherless, a defender of widows is God in His holy habitation."* (Psalm 68:5, King James Version)

14. *"For Jacob My servant's sake, and Israel Mine elect, I have even called thee by thy name: I have surnamed thee, though thou hast not known Me."* (Isaiah 45:4, King James Version)

15. *"And if children, then heirs; heirs of God, and joint-heirs with Christ if so be that we suffer with Him, that we may be also glorified together."* (Romans 8:17, King James Version)

16. *"I am your Creator. You were in My care even before you were born. Israel, don't be terrified! You are My chosen servant, My very favorite."* (Isaiah 44:2, Contemporary English Version)

17. *"From one man He made every nation of men that they should inhabit the whole earth; and He determined the times set for them and the exact places where they should live."* (Acts 17:26, New International Version)

18. *"Nothing about me is hidden from You! I was secretly woven together deep in the earth below, but with Your own eyes You saw my body being formed. Even before I was born, You had written in Your book everything I would do."* (Psalm 139:15-16, Contemporary English Version)

19. *"Long before He laid down earth's foundations, He had us in mind, had settled on us as the focus of His love, to be made whole and holy by His love. Long, long ago He decided to adopt us into His family through Jesus Christ. (What pleasure He took in planning this!) He wanted us to enter into the celebration of His lavish gift-giving by the hand of His beloved Son."* (Ephesians 1:4-6, The Message Bible)

20. *"For God so loved the world that He gave His only begotten Son, that whosoever believeth in Him should not perish, but have everlasting life."* (Saint John 3:16 King James Version)

21. *"Listen to Me, House of Jacob, all the remnant of the house of Israel, you whom I have upheld since your birth, and have carried since you were born. Even to your old age and gray hairs I am He, I am He who will sustain you. I have made you and I will carry you; I will sustain you and I will rescue you."* (Isaiah 46:3-4, Today's New International Version)

22. *"When I said, thus far you may come, but no farther, and here your proud waves must stop."* (Job 38:11 New King James Version)

23. *"But God who is rich in mercy, because of His great love with which He loved us."* (Ephesians 2:4, King James Version)

24. *"And being fully persuaded that what He had promised, He was able also to deliver."* (Romans 4:21, King James Version)

25. *"Now, O Lord God, the word which You have spoken concerning Your servant, and concerning his house, establish it forever and do as You have said."* (2 Samuel 7:25 & 1 Chronicles 17:23, New King James Version)

26. *"Thus saith the Lord, the Holy One of Israel, and his Maker, ask Me of things to come concerning My sons, and concerning the work of My hands command ye Me."* (Isaiah 45:11, King James Version)

27. *"There is a time for everything, and a season for every activity under the heavens."* (Ecclesiastics 3:1, New International Version)

28. *"Do not be anxious about anything, but in everything, by prayer and petition, with thanksgiving, present your requests to God. And the peace of God, which transcends all understanding, will guard your hearts and your minds in Christ Jesus."* (Philippians 4:6-7, New International Version)

29. *"And he said unto her, daughter, thy faith hath made thee whole; go in peace, and be whole of thy plague."* (Saint Mark 5:34, King James Version)

30. *"And He took the damsel by the hand, and said unto her, talitha cumi; which is, being interpreted, damsel, I say unto thee arise. And straightway the damsel arose and walked; for she was of the age of twelve years. And they*

were astonished with a great astonishment." (Saint Mark 5: 41-42, King James Version)

31. *"Be still, and know that I am God; I will be exalted among the nations, I will be exalted in the earth."* (Psalm 46:10. King James Version)

32. *"Be still before the Lord and wait patiently for Him fret not yourself over the one who prospers in his way, over the man who carries out evil devices!"* (Psalm 37:7, English Standard Version)

33. *"Stand in awe, and sin not: commune with your own heart upon your bed and be still."* (Psalms 4:4, King James Version)

34. *"For the vision is yet for an appointed time, but at the end it shall speak, and not lie: though it tarry, wait for it; because it will surely come, it will not tarry. Behold, his soul which is lifted up is not upright in him: But the just shall live by his faith."* (Habakkuk 2:3-4, King James Version)

35. *"The Lord God is my strength, and He will make my feet like hinds' feet, and He will make me to walk upon mine high places."* (Habakkuk 3:19, King James Version)

36. *"And when He had removed him, He raised up unto them David to be their king; to whom also He gave their testimony, and said, I have found David the son of Jesse, a man after Mine own heart, which shall fulfill all My will."* (Acts 13:22, King James Version)

37. *"The Lord hath appeared of old unto me, saying, Yea, I have loved thee with an everlasting love: therefore with loving kindness have I drawn thee."* (Jeremiah 31:3, King James Version)

38. *"My sheep listen to My voice; I know them, and they follow Me."* (Saint John 10:27, New International Version)

39. *"We all, like sheep, have gone astray, each of us has turned to our own way and the Lord has laid on Him the iniquity of us all."* (Isaiah 53:6, New International Version)

40. *They reel to and fro, and stagger like a drunken man, and are at their wit's end."* (Psalm 107:27, King James Version)

41. *"But David said to Saul, "Your servant has been keeping his father's sheep. When a lion or a bear came and carried off a sheep from the flock, I went after it, struck it and rescued the sheep from its mouth. When it turned on me, I seized it by its hair, struck it and killed it"."* (1 Samuel 17:34-35, New International Version)

42. *"We all, like sheep, have gone astray, each of us has turned to our own way; and the Lord has laid on him the iniquity of us all."* (Isaiah 53:6, New International Version)

43. *"Why are you downcast, O my soul? Why so disturbed within me?"* (Psalm 45:5, New International Version)

44. *"Yes, just as you can identify a tree by its fruit, so you can identify people by their actions."* (Saint Matthew 7:20, New Living Translation)

45. *"But the fruit of the Spirit is love, joy, peace, longsuffering, gentleness, faith, meekness, temperance".* (Galatians 5:22-23, King James Version)

46. *"For a righteous man may fall seven times and rise again, but the wicked shall fall by calamity."* (Proverbs 24:16, New King James Version)

47. *"And it happened, when Elizabeth heard the greeting of Mary, that the babe leaped in her womb; and Elizabeth was filled with the Holy Spirit."* (Saint Luke 1:41, New King James Version)

48. *"And looking at Jesus as He walked, he said, Behold the Lamb of God!"* (Saint John 1:36, New King James Version)

49. *"He must increase, but I must decrease."* (Saint John 3:30, New King James Version)

50. *"Seeing then that we have a great High Priest who has passed through the heavens, Jesus the Son of God, let us hold fast our confession. For we do not have a High Priest who cannot sympathize with our weaknesses, but was in*

all points tempted as we are, yet without sin." (Hebrews 4:14-15, New King James Version)

51. *"They said to Him, "Teacher, this woman was caught in adultery, in the very act"."* (Saint John 8:4, New King James Version)

52. *"The man who commits adultery with another man's wife, he who commits adultery with his neighbor's wife, the adulterer and the adulteress, shall surely be put to death."* (Leviticus 20:10, New King James Version)

53. *"And when He had made an end of speaking with him on Mount Sinai, He gave Moses two tablets of stone, written with the finger of God."* (Exodus 31:18, King James Version)

54. *"In the same hour the fingers of a man's hand appeared and wrote opposite the lampstand on the plaster of the wall of the king's palace; and the king saw the part of the hand that wrote."* (Daniel 5:5, New King James Version)

55. *"So Gad came to David and said to him, thus says the Lord: choose for yourself, either three years of famine, or three months to be defeated by your foes with the sword of your enemies overtaking you, or else for three days the sword of the Lord—the plague in the land, with the angel of the Lord destroying throughout all the territory of Israel. Now consider what answer I should take back to Him who sent me. And David said to Gad, I am in great distress. Please let me fall into the hand of the Lord, for His mercies are very great; but do not let me fall into the hand of man."* (1 Chronicles 21: 11-13, New King James Version):

56. *"The Lord is not slack concerning His promise, as some count slackness, but is longsuffering toward us, not willing that any should perish but that all should come to repentance."* (2 Peter 3:9, New King James Version)

57. *"For He made Him who knew no sin to be sin for us, that we might become the righteousness of God in Him."* (2 Corinthians 5:21, New King James Version)

58. *"Therefore we also, since we are surrounded by so great a cloud of witnesses, let us lay aside every weight, and the sin which so easily ensnares us, and let*

us run with endurance the race that is set before us." (Hebrews 12:1, New King James Version)

59. *"For surely there is a hereafter and your hope will not be cut off."* (Proverbs 23:18, New King James Version)

60. *"This day I call the heavens and the earth as witnesses against you that I have set before you life and death, blessings and curses. Now choose life, so that you and your children may live."* (Deuteronomy 30:19, New International Version).

61. *"Now I saw a new heaven and a new earth, for the first heaven and the first earth had passed away. Also there was no more sea."* (Revelation 21:1, New King James Version)

62. *"His lord said unto him, well done, good and faithful servant: enter thou into the joy of thy Lord."* (Saint Matthew 25:23, King James Version)

63. *"That you may be sons of your Father in heaven; for He makes His sun rise on the evil and on the good, and sends rain on the just and on the unjust."* (Saint Matthew 5:45, King James Version)

64. *"Whoever does not love does not know God, because God is love."* (1 John 4:8, New International Version)

65. *"As the Father loved Me, I also have loved you; abide in My love. If you keep My commandments, you will abide in My love, just as I have kept My Father's commandments and abide in His love."* (Saint John 15:9-10, New King James Version)

66. *"The thief does not come except to steal, and to kill, and to destroy. I have come that they may have life and that they may have it more abundantly."* (Saint John 10:10, New King James Version)

67. *"In Him was life, and the life was the light of men."* (Saint John 1:4, New King James Version)

68. *"Therefore, if anyone is in Christ, he is a new creation; old things have passed away; behold, all things have become new."* (2 Corinthians 5:17, New King James Version)

69. *"I press toward the goal for the prize of the upward call of God in Christ Jesus."* (Philippians 3:14, New King James Version)

70. *"Here I am! I stand at the door and knock. If anyone hears my voice and opens the door, I will come in and eat with him, and he with me."* (Revelation 3:20, New International Version)

71. *"I say unto you that likewise there will be more joy in heaven over one sinner who repents than over ninety-nine just persons who need no repentance."* (Saint Luke 15:7, King James Version)